Creation Science
Children's Church
Lesson Plans

By
Helena Cromwell

Creation Science Children's Church Lesson Plans

Author: Helena Cromwell

Copyright © 2013 owned by Helena Cromwell

Publisher: Cross Wise Publishing
http://crosswisepublishing.com

ISBN- 978-0692227237
ISBN- 0692227237

This guide is dedicated to the many students and teachers of the faith who desire to refute the awful lie told by so called, "evolution scientist".

May you find this guide to be a great starting point for sharing the true story regarding how the world and universe was, in fact created by God Almighty.

"If the devil can reduce God's Magnificent Creation to a Meaningless glob, then he's Dancing a jig"

Anonymous

More Learning & Motivation Ideas
http://crosswisepublishing.com

Introduction

This book is a compilation of lessons the author used in her own classroom over the past several years. It is designed to reduce teacher preparation time, while ramping up student learning experiences.

The author believes the Bible to be the infallible word of God, and that the world was created in the time and manner in which the book of Genesis records. Further, she is greatly concerned about the false indoctrination of evolution through the educational system, and believes that people of faith need to be made aware of the threat that evolution brings to those who believe in Bible principles.

Helena Cromwell is convinced that so called, evolution 'science' has and will continue to play a major role in bringing Mathew 24:24 to pass. It is true that "...if it were possible, they shall deceive the very elect". Helena feels an urgency to equip teachers to educate young students in Creation Science principles in order to combat the false doctrine of evolution.

A concerted effort has been made to present each lesson in a methodical manner, so as to lighten the teacher's load as much as possible. Helena realizes that one of the major stumbling blocks to volunteer teaching staff is lesson preparation time. Therefore, she has tried to prepare the way in a simple and straightforward way as possible

Table of Contents

God Was Organized

Wonderful Water

God Created Light

Separating The Firmament (Atmosphere)

God Brings Life to The World He Created

God Created Us

How Life Began Part 1

How Life Began Part 2

The Question Evolution Cannot Answer

Sign Language Night

After His/Her Kind

God, Our Creator

Miracles – God's Supernatural Power

Life is in The Blood

Evolution & Creation are both Points of View

Toddler Challenge

Dot-to-Dot Christmas Mural

Supplemental Pages

God IS Organized

Beginning Activity: Demonstrate how being organized is better than being disorganized. (Have someone organize letters, numbers, money)
We're going to play a game. Who wants to be FIRST?

FIRST means, "In the Beginning". That means in order.

No Plan: Start the game by making a random mark on the board and tell each child to add to it. After everyone has had a turn, ask the kids to tell us what they see. (Different people will see different things).

All agree there are observable marks
Not all will agree what they mean
Whose idea is the most important? (Nobody's idea is more important than anyone else's) So, we start looking for answers.

Where can we find answers?

One person says it looks like a flower.
One person says it looks like a blob of nothing.

We must RESEARCH to find the answer.

Which research tools might we use?
1. Bible
2. Science Book
3. Microscope
4. Experts (people who know more than we do).

Have the kids vote on the meaning of the drawing.

Something?   Nothing? Possibly Something???

Now do the Pattern again starting it off with a Plan. We're going to draw a tree. Make a mark that would begin a tree trunk. Let each student help finish it.

Comparing the two pictures, ask, "Which picture is Best" the picture with a plan, or the one without a plan?

> Everything you see around you is made with a Plan. Before He even began His Creation, God had a plan for the World, for the Plants, the Animals, and the People.

The first tool you can use to solve a problem is, your own two eyes. Look around you and you will see God's plan in everything. The tiniest germ is made up from an organized plan. Germs help protect us. There are thousands of germs in your guts that help protect your body. Those tiny little germs or bacteria help your body digest food.

We see that God has a PLAN for everything and everyone. Our bodies, our world and even our Air is highly organized.

It makes no sense to think that unorganized is as good as organized.

Creation is Organized	Evolution is Unorganized
1. God Said/God Saw	By Chance/(Nobody Saw)
	No pattern/direction

Scripture Look Up:
1 Corinthians 14:40
Jeremiah 29:11

Pair the children up in sets of 2. Each one can look up a scripture and read it to the other one. Ask them to listen for these words: *Order* and *Plans*. When they hear that word they can raise their hand to let you know they found it. Place a small treat in each child's hand as a reward for following directions.

Game Time: Organizing
1. Give each child a small container full of nickels, dimes, pennies and quarters
2. Ask them to use their own imagination to "organize" the money
3. Once they have completed their assignment walk around and let them explain their idea to you.
4. You may even take a photo of them and their "creation" to validate their creativity

The object of this exercise is to show the kids that even if, by some mathematically impossible chance, all the pieces to a complex system like these coins were to actually be present; it would still take outside intervention to create a purposeful product/pattern.

If you want to ramp up the game you can do the following:

5. Have two teams race to "organize" the money
6. The first team to finish runs over and rings a bell.
   Repeat the Game.

   Note: We were amazed at how diverse our kids' ideas of how to organize the coins were. Some stacked the money based on its economic value; some organized it according to its size and others formed patterns resembling flowers, animals or people. Yet others separated the coins according to colors or year stamped on their coins.

Wonderful Water

Beginning Activity:

1. Get a measuring cup that shows ounces.
2. Let each child pour up 2 ounces of water in the measuring cup and transfer it into a Ziploc baggie.
3. Put the Baggies into the freezer.

Review:

1. Name 2 kinds of Scientist (Evolution & Creation)
2. Which are we?
3. Where do look for Creation Facts?
   Bible + Science Observations & Experiments = Truth
4. Where is first clue to Creation Facts Found?
5. Old T. or New T.

Scripture Look Up:

Genesis 1:1-6 Genesis 2:7 and Isaiah 40: 12 & 13

1. Which Verse Tells about H2o?
2. Which Verse Tells about Land?
3. Which Verse gives us clues about how Powerful God is?

God created the world with order and purpose
1. Did God create the water or the fish first?
2. Wouldn't it have been ridiculous for Him to create the fish first? (Using a gold fish and fish bowl ask a student to take the fish out of the tank and just hold it)
3. Do you think the fish would have liked it if God created Him first? Why?
(Put the fish back into the tank)

Lets Talk About Water
God put 2 kinds of water on the earth
1. Saltwater for the Oceans where the fish live
2. Freshwater for land where people live
Can you name a fish that can live both places?
Salmon.

Evolution science says that people actually began in the ocean and then became people and moved to the land.

Creation science says that people were formed from the ground. The Bible says that God formed man from the "dust of the ground" Gen. 2:7

People cannot drink ocean water, but they can drink land water. Why?

All the minerals in our body, like iron, zinc, copper and calcium, are also found in the ground.

Does it sound to you like people came from the ocean or from the land like God says?

The Bible says that when people die their body returns to dust. All scientists agree. All that's left of people at the graveyard is just their bones, and even the bones crumble after a long time.

Let's make Pretend Earths

Materials: One Blue piece of felt cut into a circle, for each child, dirt and glue. Blow dryer (use on low) to dry glue

1. Using a large needle stitch all the way around the edge of the felt with a strong thread – maybe even flossing string.
2. Make a draw string bag by pulling the two ends of your thread, but leave a large enough hole for the sand/dirt to be spooned into the bag
3. Fill the bag and tie it off
4. Form the bag into a round "earth". We had to do additional stitching to form a nice round earth.

Talk to the kids about how important it might be for them to mark their "earth" so other people will know they are the one who made it. God wants us to remember that HE made our world also.

Save the earth for future lessons when twigs and grass and other things can be added/glued on. Later, using the blue color to represent oceans students may want to draw pictures of fish out in the, "Ocean".

Let's Talk More About Water

1. Scientist believes that all living things need liquid water to survive.
2. Human bodies can live for weeks without food, but only days without water.
3. Have you ever seen a plant die because someone forgot to water it?
4. Water comes in 3 forms: liquid, solid, gas
5. The earth is the only planet in our solar system to have liquid water.

Now, Let's go back to the freezer and finish our water experiment.

1. Let the kids get their Baggies out and put the frozen water in the microwave to melt the ice.
2. Using a skillet let each child pour their water into the skillet
3. The teacher will now boil the water away on a burner and turn the water to a vapor/gas.
4. Explain to the children that the water in lakes, rivers and oceans vaporize into the atmosphere and ends up in the air and is recycled over and over again through rain and snow that falls back down to the ground.
5. In fact we just use the same water over and over again that was here from the beginning of time.

6. The earth cleans the water and makes it reusable. You may be drinking water someone took a bath in over a hundred years ago.
7. Don't worry; it's been washed pure by the earth.

Game Time: Sit in a circle, toss the ball and the one to catch it must finish this sentence.

Without water we wouldn't have _____

You will need the following supplies:

Baggies
Blue Balloons
Plastic Funnels
Dirt
Glue
Blow Dryers
Gold Fish
Fish Bowl
World Globe

God Created Light
"God said, let there be light and there was light and God saw the light that it was good: and god divided the light from the darkness" Genesis 1:3&4

Lesson Objectives:
1. To show kids how Brilliant God is. When He makes a simple statement like, "it was good" we need to understand that what is simply "good" to God, passes our definition of Magnificent!
2. Light Illuminates (shines)
3. Light Radiates (origin of energy/heat)

Place as many different types of light sources as you can think of on display for the students. (Flashlight, different kinds of light bulbs, candle, match, picture of a firefly, lightening bolt, camp fire, street light etc.)

Beginning Activity: Have the kids make a LIGHT SOURCE mural by using a long roll of paper tapped on the worktable. They can draw and color anything they can think of that would be a light source.

Scripture Look Up: Students will look up scriptures (using the concordance/index) in their Bibles that talk about light and reference them on the mural. You can display the mural in the hall or an area where passersby can view it.

God created: LIGHT Source and He Saw that it was good - Genesis 1:3, 4 & 5. This was NOT the sun, moon or stars! Those light sources came on the 4th day. Light was the property from which God created the sun, moon and stars. (Like buying fabric but making the shirt a few days later)

God then divided the Light from the DARKNESS and He created TIME – evening & morning = Day

What is Light? – Light is radiant energy. Science agrees that a basic law of physics states that the world is made up of **Time, Space and Matter (stuff).** Light is the driving force that maintains Time, Space and Stuff.

Do we Really Need Light?

We Need Light to:
1. See
2. Plants need to grow
3. Body gets Vitamin D from the sun
4. God gave us Light so we could_____ and
   _____

He divided the light from the darkness so we could_____
Do we need darkness? Why?

Cover the windows with white paper, and then tape a black trash bag over the whole window.

Turn the light out and ask them what they see. Darkness is what existed upon the earth before God created Light.

Now, remove the black trash bags and ask them if they can see better. Why can you see better (because there is light out in the hallway.) The point is that God created light before he created the sun, moon and stars.

Scientist tell us that there are untold Galaxies out in outer space with endless number of stars. They call the sun a Star. Lets pretend that in here is our galaxy, and out there is the other galaxies. What is the name of our galaxy? (Everyone gets a milky way when we play our game)

Turn the light on and re-read Genesis1:3 & 4 God divided the Light from the darkness.

FUN FACTS ABOUT LIGHT
http://www.sciencekids.co.nz/sciencefacts/light.html

- In physics, light refers to electromagnetic radiation. The light we normally talk about in everyday life refers to the visible spectrum (the part of the electromagnetic spectrum that the human eye can see).

Animals can see parts of the spectrum that humans can't. For example, a large number of insects can see ultraviolet (UV) light.

UV light can be used to show things the human eye can't see, coming in handy for forensic scientists.

The wavelength of infrared light is too long to be visible to the human eye.

Scientists study the properties and behaviors of light in a branch of physics known as optics.

Isaac Newton observed that a thin beam of sunlight hitting a glass prism on an angle creates a band of visible colors that includes red, orange, yellow, green, blue, indigo and violet (ROYGBIV). This occurred because different colors travel through glass (and other things) at different speeds, causing them to refract at different angles and separate from each other. (When God created light He created the rainbow at the same time – people just didn't see it until the sky had water to separate it's colors)

Light travels very, very fast. The speed of light in a vacuum (an area empty of matter) is around 186,000 miles per second (300,000 kilometres per second).

Light travels slower through different things such as glass, water and air. Light travels through glass faster than it does through water, and faster through air because air has less refractive index to slow it down.

Light takes 1.255 seconds to get from the Earth to the Moon.

Sunlight can reach a depth of around 80 metres (262 feet) in the ocean.

Photosynthesis is a process that involves plants using energy from sunlight to convert carbon dioxide into food.

Experiments 1
1. What you'll need to show how light radiates heat:

One or more hand sized rocks and a gooseneck lamp

Instructions:

Let the students hold the rock to verify its temp

Put the rock under the lamp and leave 20 minutes

Have a student verify the rock is warmer

• tWhat's happening?
Light radiates heat and the rock (the world) absorbs and retains the heat.

Experiment 2. Show how we normally cant see ultraviolet light with the naked eye

You'll need a $20 bill
Someone's drivers license
Black light

Hold the light over the $20 to reveal the hidden strip on the end

Hold the light over the drivers license to reveal the hidden markings

Experiment 3: Show how light bends

Using a laser light point across the room to show that light will travel a great distance

Punch a hole ¼ way up a 2liter soda bottle. Fill it with water.

Shine the laser on the opposite side of the hole and watch how the light follows the water instead of going straight.

God Created Light
"God said, let there be light and there was light and God saw the light that it was good: and God divided the light from the darkness" Genesis 1:3&4

Answer This

1. When did light begin?

2. What might have happened if God hadn't divided the Light from the Darkness?

3. What is your favorite light?

4. Is there a bad light?

5. What would happen if light were suddenly taken away from us?

6. Do you agree with God that light is "good"?

7. Fill in the Blank. God's invention of Light is

   Absolutely _____

Separating the "FIRMAMENT"
(Atmosphere)

Beginning Activity: Complete the Creation Maze/Color Picture that demonstrates the earth's equator.

The air we breathe is what is known as the Atmosphere. God created air because He knew people, plants and animals would need air to breathe, and wind to cool us down. Genesis 1:6, 7, 8 (Which day was the atmosphere made in? 2nd)

Air has 3 parts mixed together: (Make **3 Paper Costumes.** On the O2 draw a heart, liver, brain and hand. Have the kids that wear the costumes to lock their arms together and walk around the room). Although we breathe in all three gases we really only use one and that is o2. Our lungs are wonderfully made to not accept Nitrogen or Argon into our blood streams.

1. N -itrogen
2. O –xygen (visits all the cells in the body)
3. A –rgon
4. H

N-O-A-H spells Noah, but we take the H away

Which of these three do our bodies need to live?

The atmosphere doesn't float off the earth due to "gravity". Gravity holds the atmosphere down to where we can breathe. Drop toy off a **ladder** to demo gravity.

The atmosphere is also like an insulation blanket spread around the earth. It keeps us from getting too hot and too cold.

In Genesis 1:6-8 scripture explains how simple it was for God to make our atmosphere; nonetheless, the atmosphere's relationship to life in our solar system is more complex than even most scientist realize.

Have each child name the 3 air gasses for a reward.

The Jet Stream plays a vital role in our weather. It is what causes the wind to travel throughout the world.

3,000 years ago In Ecclesiastes 1:6 the Jet Stream was declared, however it wasn't until WWII that an airmen confirmed its existence. Use **ribbon** to demonstrate the jet stream on the earth.

Do the Atmospheric Pressure Experiment Here

Scripture Look Up

On the 3rd day God created
The Oceans, The Land and The Plants
Lets Read Genesis 1:9-13

World map (Have the kids color the map and the younger ones color the animals)

Hand Art:

Have each child draw its hand on a blue sheet of paper. On each finger write one of the 5 Oceans in the World. Designed to help them remember there are 5 Oceans.
1. Pacific Ocean
2. Atlantic Ocean
3. Indian Ocean
4. Arctic Ocean
5. Southern Ocean (designated as an official ocean in 2000 by the International Hydrographic Organization)

Directions for part 2 of our Earth Project;

1. **Spread out newspaper on tables**
2. **Draw the North American Continent on the newly made cloth Worlds**
3. **Smear glue for land on earth projects**
4. **Pin-prick the cloth so dirt falls onto the glue.**
5. **Use more glue to build up the land mass**
6. **Add vegetation if available**

May use blow dryers to dry the glue if needed

2 Atmospheric Pressure Experiments

There's positive pressure and negative pressure. When we breathe in – we're using negative pressure, and when you exhale (blow the air out) that is using positive pressure. Negative pressure pulls air in and positive pressure pushes air. Our nervous system, called the autonomic (meaning automatic) nervous system is activated automatically to breathe in fresh air when the CO_2 (a toxic gas) starts to build up in our blood stream.

1st Experiment

Need:

Water
Large paper plate
Candle
Match
1 oz. water
Medium Pickle Jar

1. Place the candle onto the paper plate and light it.
2. Place the dry pickle jar over the candle and wait for the candle to go out (this forms a negative pressure)
3. Grasp the jar firmly and try to life it off the paper plate
4. Set the paper plate and pour the water around the outside of the jar
5. In a few minutes the negative pressure will loose it's vacuum and suck the water inside

2nd Experiment
Supplies:
Large Juice Bottle
Balloon
Suction Apparatus (syringe)

1. Make a small hole in the Juice bottle (I used a metal clothes hanger and burned it in)
2. Place the balloon inside the bottle and stretch the opening over the opening of the bottle
3. Ask for a volunteer to try to blow the balloon up
4. Now, pull the air out of the bottle through the small hole by either sucking it out, or pulling it out with a syringe
5. After the balloon is inflated hold your finger over the hole to maintain the negative pressure that's inside the bottle
6. When you release your finger the pressure equalizes and the balloon will deflate

What's happening is that the pressure on the inside of the bottle is now negative and the negative pressure is pulling in the air from outside of the bottle into the balloon.

God brings Life to the World He Created

Beginning Activity: Use boxes of Kleenex and floral wire to make paper flowers for mothers

Scripture Look Up: Genesis 1: 9-13

Ask: Why did God give us plants?
1. Food source
2. They absorb carbon dioxide and give off Oxygen that's why we need the forest
3. They are pretty

Ask: How should we take care of plants inside the house?
1. (plants breathe at night so if you have lots of plants inside your house, you need to provide them plenty of atmosphere at night like using a humidifier)
2. Put them by a window so they can get some sunshine

Lets name some plants we like to eat

Lets name some plants we don't like to eat

Did you know that some plants actually eat meat? They eat small birds, insects and flies.

For example, (show pictures of) Venus Fly Trap, bladderworts, butterworts, pitcher plants and sundews. Many pictures available throughout the internet,.

Scientist estimates that there are bout 350,000 species of plants living on the earth. Only 288,000 have names.

Plants have many parts. Basically, Chlorophyll is what makes plants green and allows them to absorb sunlight so they can produce their own food.

Additionally, the cell walls of a plant are made of cellulose. Unlike animals plants cannot move from one place to the other on their own.

Question: Why did God make the plants before people?

Genesis 1: 29 & 30 says that God gave us plants for "meat". Why did God give us *plants* for meat? That seems weird. (Because before sin there was no blood shed, and for us to use animals as meat there must be blood shed).

Both people and animals use plants for food. Without plants there would be no life on earth.

Flowering plants reproduce/make new plants through the use of seeds and a process called pollination.

Moss and ferns reproduce through spores. Although spores are unicellular or one-cell organisms they actually have both the mother and father locked up together inside the cell.

Once they break free and the wind blows them back together their children spores start the cycle all over again, and we have more spores.

When God said unto them, "Be fruitful, and multiply, and replenish the earth", Genesis 1:28 He was talking to all the future mothers and fathers in the world.

Although, sometimes the steps to becoming parents that plants or animals take may seem a little strange to us, God designed plants, animals, and humans all to reproduce both boys and girls in one way or the other.

People, plants and animals did not come from just a one-celled amoeba (that somehow eventually became the mother and father of people, plants and animals) like evolutionists say.

Flowering plants provide:
1. Food
2. Drinks
3. Clothes
4. Medicine

Activities:

- Look at a plant under the microscope

- Plant some seeds and send home with children
  God Creates the Sun, Moon and Stars!
Look Up: Genesis 1: 14-19

Scripture says what science just found out. The stars are not all the same. They're different size and shapes 1 Cor. 15:41.

The Bible also says that God calls the stars by name. Psalms 147:4.

There are estimated to be between 100 and 400 billion stars in the Milky Way galaxy alone. Can anyone write 400 billion?
1,000,000,000,000, one million million, 10^{12} = 1 billion X 400

Activity

Using glow in the dark stars create a star system for the kids to enjoy when the lights are turned out.

Tell the children that scientist believe the Sun is really a huge star that we can only see in the daytime. Tonight we're studying stars we only see at night.

Comparing Real Stars to Manmade Stars
Turn the lights out to show the pre-hung glow in the dark stars. Now go outside. Ask, who votes for manmade stars? Who votes for God made stars?

Return to the classroom for a game.

Game Time: Creation "Who or What Am i?

WHAT YOU WILL DO:
Divide the children into two or more teams. Choose a student to be it. The object of the game is to be the first team to guess which creation the teacher has selected. Children can only ask questions that can be answered with yes or no. Teams take turns asking questions until the correct person, animal or thing has been named or time runs out.

If children need help getting started the teacher may suggest that teams ask questions such as:

- Can I be found in the Old Testament?
- Can I be found in Genesis?
- Am I a man?
- Am I a woman?
- Am I a light?
- Do people drink me?
- Am I a plant?
- Was I created on the first day?
- Did God create me last? Do I swim in the ocean?

- Apple tree
- Ant
- Moon
- Star
- Sun
- Ocean
- Salmon
- Bear
- Rose
- Wind or Air
- Dirt
- Water
- Bible

God Created Us
in His own image, and with his own
"Hands"
Genesis 1:27 and Genesis 2:7

This lesson will begin a short series emphasizing the miracle of God creating people.

The creation of the human body, soul and spirit is an awesome subject, and one that should be studied more in depth.

Today's lesson discusses the human hand. How it can be used for good, but also we'll discuss the ramifications of the hand that reached out and took the fruit from the tree of good and evil in the garden of Eden. Genesis 3:6.

Emphasize how important it is for us to make good choices, and how we must rule over our hands so we use them only for good.

Open with Prayer

Beginning Activity: Show the craft tree so the children will have an example to follow as they build their Tree of Good and Evil. Provide each child with 3 pieces of construction paper. Instruct them to use the brown/green to draw their hands onto the paper for the tree trunk. Provide glue and a second piece to glue the tree trunk to. Use the last piece for them to cut or tear in to pieces to make the forbidden fruit for their tree.

Talk about the miracle of the hand. It's construction, function and placement on our bodies, and the fact that our thumb can touch the end of all 4 of our finger pads. This is extremely important because it gives us a greater ability to grasp and control very small tools such as being able to use both sewing needles and thimbles at the same time. This is only one of many advantages that God fore saw that humans would need in their lives that animals would not. **We are not an evolutionary process.**

In apes and Old World monkeys, the thumbs can be rotated around its axis, but the extensive area of contact between the pulps of the thumb and index finger is *exclusively* a human characteristic.[19]   *Wikipedia.*

For example, since apes were not created with the ability to know the difference between good and evil they didn't sin. Therefore, they never became naked. They would never have a need to sew them selves clothes to wear.

People, on the other "hand" were CREATED from the very beginning with the ability to gain the knowledge of good and evil. Scripture tells us that Adam & Eve were created with the dexterity necessary to "sew fig leaves together" Genesis 3:7. They didn't have to wait millions of years.

Our thumbs did NOT evolve (as evolutionist would have us believe). Evolutionists have absolutely **NO proof** that people came from Apes. Our thumbs alone prove that, from the beginning God made humans and apes different.

Scripture Look Up:

Have students look up scriptures in their Bibles as the lesson progresses beginning with Genesis 1:27 and 2:7.

Now ask students to write/tell something good they could do with their hands palms down. For example: Acts 28:8 (we can pray for each other.)

Now ask the students to write/tell something good they could do with their hands with their palms turned up. For example discuss: Matthew 14:31.

Jesus reached out his hand and saved someone who was in trouble, and his hand still reaches for us today. John 3:16 - 18

Another of Jesus' miracles involved a man's hand. Read Matthew 12:9-15

When people go in to testify in court they are asked to raise their right hand and swear an oath to tell the truth. That custom comes straight from the Bible. Read Isaiah 62:8.

1. God's promises: Psalms 91:7
2. Victory in the LORD our God:
   Psalm118:16
3. God's hand is not short: Isaiah 59:1
4. God holds us in the palm of his hand.
   Isaiah 49:15,16

Game Time:
No Hands Relay Races:
1. Form 2 teams.
2. At one end of the room is 4 chairs.
3. Two chairs hold 3 balloons.
4. Two chairs are empty.
5. Teams will line up to race against each other to the chairs with the balloons.
6. The object of the game is for each team member to transport all 3 of the balloons from one chair to the other without using their hands.
7. Then they will run back to their team, tag their team the next player (not using their hands) and the next team member will race down to move the balloons back to the original chair.
8. If they drop a balloon they have to pick it up without using their hands.
9. Continue until all the team members have had a chance to move balloons

Isn't it awesome that God gave us hands?

Repeat the game if time permits

End with treats.

How Life Began Part 1

Opening Prayer: Ask a student (possibly the one who misbehaved in the last session) to ask God's blessing upon our class.

Beginning Activity: We all began as a baby – scientifically called an embryo. The size of that baby started out about the size of a dot. (Make a dot on a piece of paper and hold it up). Inside that dot is 6 ft. of DNA.

We're going to call **DNA – Do Not Argue** because it gives the orders of what color our skin, hair, and eyes will be. It tells if we are going to be a boy or girl and how tall we will grow to be. Those orders will never be changed naturally. Some babies start out with white or blonde hair and their hair eventually becomes brown, but if a baby is red headed or has black hair it will always be a red head or black haired person until it is old and gray. IF we are born with black skin, then we will always have black skin. That is God's plan for us. Our DNA decides all those things.

Beginning Activity: Watch this short 5 minute video

https://www.youtube.com/watch?v=CBeCxKzYiIA

The embryo of a baby starts out about the size of a dot. Inside that dot is 6 ft. of DNA.

Scripture Look Up: Have students look up and read Psalms 139:13-18

The Bible says that God chose Mary to be Jesus' mother. Some religions teach that children choose who their parents will be. I don't know if we really choose our parents, but I do know that they are the ones who pass their DNA along to us, and God says we should always love and respect them.

The Bible says in Ephesians 6:1 Children, **obey** your parents in the Lord: for this is right.

Craft Time:

You will need to demonstrate this prior to passing out the paper plates. Make DNA samples. Take paper plates and cut the edges off. Begin cutting ½ inches from the sides and keep cutting in circles until you're all the way to the middle. Repeat with another plate. Now use colored construction paper cut into strips to make the "DNA LADDER"... Use the yellow, green, red and blue colors of construction paper to make the strips. Glue, tape or staple the strips onto the two-paper plate strips to form the double helix DNA ladder.

For my group I drew circular lines on each paper plate to help them stay on course. The point is to make a spiral.

NATURAL SELECTION GAME

Because many evolution scientists point to natural selection as proof of evolution it is important the students be made aware of the limitations of natural selection. A simple, yet impactful game, designed to show how illogical it is to make the assumption that natural selection adds DNA (resulting in molecules to man), is available in the supplemental portion of this manual.

How Life Began Part 2

Prayer: You may want to ask one of the students to open with prayer. I often ask the student who misbehaved the most at the previous session to open in prayer and direct them to ask God to help us learn more about Him.

Beginning Activity:

This week we're going to do some painting and an experiment, so everyone will need to put his or her lab coats and safety glasses on.

Using watercolors have the children paint a self-portrait. (You may want to draw a basic girl/boy drawing for them to build upon.) Tell them to think about how fearfully and wonderfully they are made. They can paint the color of their hair, skin, eyes, heart, blood type, height, weight, freckles, happy gene, smart gene and temper. All different colors can be used to add a little imagination to the project.

The one part of ourselves that we can't paint is our spirit and that is something evolution scientist can't explain. Genesis 2: 7

Scripture Look Up: While our pictures dry lets see what the Bible has to say about how we are made. Genesis 2:7, Isaiah 44:24, Job 10:11, 12 Hebrews 11:3 Proverbs 8: 22 -27

Discussion: Hold up one of the DNA helixes from last week. Review what DNA is (a large coiled mollycule) and what it does (DNA orders that tell the cells in our bodies what color to make our hair, eyes, skin and so on).

How many feet of DNA is in the initial dot that babies start out as? 6ft.

In our experiment today we're going to be separating fat molecules that are floating around in milk and cream. We expect the more fat molecules there are to be separated the longer it will take. So, lets go check out our hypothesis.

Experiment:

Pair the students into teams of 2. Give each student a plate to pour his or her respective milk solution into.

One students get the half and half, and the other student gets the low fat milk.

Both students get a q-tip they will dip into the Dawn Soap solution. They can share the dish soap plate, and food coloring.

Explain that we use dish soap to wash our dishes with because soap breaks up fat, greasy molecules left on our dishes.

In this experiment we're going to watch the fat molly – cules get separated before our eyes.

Since we don't have a microscope, we will use food coloring to track the path that fat molly – cules take.

Suppplies;

Dawn Dish Soap
Half & half cream
Low fat milk
Food coloring
q-tips
Small Paper plates
Labels

Demonstrate the following Process then allow the children to perform their own experiments

Step one – pour the assigned 2 ounces of milk onto the paper plate

Step two – pick 2 food-coloring bottles

Step Three – put 2 drops of each color into the middle of the milk solution side by side

Step Four – dip the q-tip into the soap and stand it up in the center of the solution

The fat molecules will spread at 2 different rates – according to how much fat is in each solution

Ask the students to determine which specimen finished moving first? Ask if they know why one finished faster. (The more fat there is to move the longer it will take)

Ask them if they know why God gave people and animals fat molecules?

Ask: Who has the most fat molecules in their body - men or women? (Answer: Women – fat is needed to grow and feed healthy babies. A baby's brain grows very fast its first year of life. The mother's milk has been scientifically proven to have just the right amount of fat to make sure the baby grows a healthy brain. God gave men more muscles than women so they could hunt and gather food for the mother, father and older children).

God made men to be strong so they can protect their families.

(The closer we look at how highly organized God made our bodies, the more we realize it is ridiculous to believe that we are accidental beings that evolved from some unknown source.) Even secular scientist marvel at the complexity of the human body.

The Question Evolution Cannot Answer
(But, the Bible Can)

Ask a student to open with Prayer:

Ask: Who would like to know the BIGGEST question that evolution scientist cannot answer, but creation scientist can answer? (Hold the answer for later)

Beginning Activity: Open by writing the words to this little song on the marker board and singing it: READ John 11:25,26

> *I'm gonna live forever, I'm gonna die no never, Jesus died on a tree for me, and I'm gonna live Forever…* **Found on Youtube.**

https://search.yahoo.com/search;_ylt=AjR1g5zd.ER SDW69ZLRU9pW.ul6?p=I%27m+gonna+live+forev er%2C+I%27m+gonna+die+no+never+&type=2butto n&fr=ush-mailn_02

Discussion: Explain that tonight we have 2 games and 2 pieces of candy for each student who plays both games. We have to move along quickly to get to both games, so everyone needs to listen and work quickly or the last game will have to wait for next week.

Let's talk about what it means to become a Living Soul.

Hold up an empty balloon. Show the students how it has a form, but it's empty so it can only lay flat and isn't much fun.

Engage the misbehaving student by having them read Genesis 2:7.

Ask if anyone knows what a nostril is?

Say, "Everyone stand up and take a really deep breath through your nostril"

God gave us air to breathe and nostrils to breathe it with, and lungs and red blood cells to maintain the breath of life in our bodies.

Optional: Explain how oxygen flows around the body attached to the hemoglobin of a red blood cell. Demonstrate by placing 2 pieces of masking tape – side by side – on the floor to make an imaginary blood vein. Using construction papers make an organ (heart, lungs, liver, pancreas, kidneys etc.) to be taped onto each student for full class participation. (Make an RBC costume by stapling 2 large red poster boards together – leave an opening for the head). Color one side of the poster board darker to represent the hemoglobin. Pick a student to don the costume to pretend they are a red blood cell. Attach a piece of candy onto the hemoglobin area of the RBC to represent the hitchhiking oxygen molecule. Have students line up along the blood vein. As the RBC passes by, each student/organ will pull a piece of candy/o2 molecule off the RBC and consume it. (The RBC should walk slowly so each student/organ can retrieve their share of the candy/oxygen). Tell the children to take a seat as soon as they have taken their portion. Otherwise, if you prefer, just draw the process on the marker board.

Talk about how that before man had the breath of life breathed into him, he was just like the balloon. He just laid there flat and couldn't move.

Blow up the balloon and begin to interact with it.

Once man became a living soul, with the breath of life that God gave him, he was able to move, and work and play, but more importantly, man was able to talk to God.

Ask the students "What is a Soul"?

Explain that God created us and gave us an eternal, "living soul".

Our soul is the most precious thing we own. If we have asked Jesus to forgive us of our sins it is the part of us that goes to heaven when we die.
Ask:

> Raise your hand if you want to go to heaven when you die?

1. What must we do to make sure we're going to heaven when we die?
2. Let's pray and ask Jesus to forgive our sins and be our savior and friend so that when we die we can go to heaven. (Pray the Sinners prayer and have the children repeat it after you.)

SCRIPTURE LOOK UP

Deuteronomy 6:5

And thou shalt **love the Lord thy God** with all thine heart, and with all **thy soul**, and with all **thy** might.

Matthew 22:

37 Jesus said unto him, Thou shalt love the Lord thy God with all thy heart, and with all thy soul, and with all thy mind.

38 This is the first and great commandment.

39 And the second is like unto it, Thou shalt love thy neighbor as thyself.

Ecclesiastes 12:7 (NKJV) Then the dust will return to the earth as it was, And the spirit will return to God who gave it.

Take a large tray and fill it with different kinds of fruit. In the middle of the tray put a chocolate candy bar for each child.

Tell the children they can take anything they want off the tray. (Most will likely pick a candy bar)

As the children are having their snack ask them if they want to know the answer to the BIGGEST question that evolution scientist cannot explain, but creation scientist can explain?

The answer is: How did people become living souls with an inborn knowledge of good and evil?

The answer to that question is found in Genesis 2:16 & 17

Once Adam & Eve ate from that tree of the knowledge of good and evil, the Bible says they let sin inside of them and it has been passed down to every person born ever since.

From that day until now whatever we let into our bodies becomes a part of us. If we take in harmful things such as _____ then we harm ourselves inside and we become weak, but if we take in healthy things like_____ then we grow stronger.

When it's game time provide a Large Balloon for each child to blow up and play this game with.

GAME TIME:

Help Me Get To Heaven – Each person is given a balloon. The balloon is their pretend soul. (they could even draw a face on it if time permits) The object of the game is to get your soul from one end of the room (earth) to the other end of the room/heaven, and into a box/the pearly gates, for safe keeping. Form 2 Teams:

First 2 contestants pick someone to race back to back with them against the other team. Each team tries to keep their Soul/balloon held safely between their backs. The person who got their soul/balloon to heaven picks someone new to help get to heaven. The game keeps going until everyone has made it to heaven. The team to get all their members to heaven first is the winner.

SIGN LANGUAGE NIGHT:
Creation for Kids
Genesis Chapter One Review

Precession: Use distiller to show kids that salt can be removed from the water using the same basic principles as rainwater.

Beginning Activity: Lets Make Rainwater;
Get a container of water and let each child add a scoop of dirt to it. Let another child stir up the solution. Pour the dirty water solution into a water distiller and turn it on. (If you don't have a distiller here is how to make a homemade one).
https://www.youtube.com/watch?v=4sqRvUzqDCE

Now, explain how natural rain is made.
When water warms up and is evaporated from saltwater (the ocean) it forms a steam cloud that leaves behind the salt. Once the cloud is really high up in the air it begins to cool off and the water stops being steam and turns back to liquid droplets. The droplets fall to the ground wherever the wind happened to blow the cloud. That is God's way of taking the salt out of ocean water and making it drinkable for humans and safe for plants and animals.

The process is: liquid water gets heated up ->
Evaporation = Gas (water vapor) then Cools Down =
Condensation into water droplets -> Gas goes back to
liquid = rain

Explain that people have figured out a machine that
can purify water in the same basic way.

At the end of class open the distiller and show the
kids the dirt in the bottom of it.

Scripture Look Up: Genesis 1 Review:

Assign the 31 verses of Genesis One among the
students. Ask each child to read their assigned verses
from chapter one as the "sign person" signs their
verse. Another student may pretend to be a mirror
and copy sign as the verse is read.

STARS
Scientists generally agree that there are between 3 and 7 x
10^{22} stars in the universe. That would amount to between
30 and 70 billion, trillion stars to brighten our world ….
Yippee!

Facts from the Bible:
1. Stars - Pslm. 147:4 & 5
2. Wind - God MADE the weight for the wind. o2 Job 28:25
3. Water - weighs the water by measure H2o

Game Time: RACE AGAINST THE CLOCK.
Form 2 teams. Tape all the balloons to a wall/object. Write the ledger below on the marker board. Using the ledger as their guide each child picks ONE balloon that they think is the right color to build the verse and then tapes their balloon to the table. (19) colors. The team to get all the balloons in the right order to complete Genesis 1:1 in the least amount of time wins.

THE = blue
BEGINNING = green
MOVED = dark blue
GOD = White
AND = yellow
WAS = orange
WITHOUT= black
 CREATED = pink
FORM = grey
DARKNESS =
FACE OF =
EARTH = brown
UPON =
HEAVENS = purple
DEEP =
 In = red
VOID =
SPIRIT =
WATERS =

If you run out of colors then use numbers instead

"AFTER HIS/THEIR KIND"
Genesis 1:11-13; 1:21; 1:24,25; 1:26-31

Opening Activity: Plant more seeds. Emphasis is on "after his kind".

DISCUSSION:
1. What are some *kinds* of plants mentioned in the Bible?
2. What are some *kinds* of fish mentioned in the Bible?
3. What are some of the *kinds* of animals mentioned in the Bible?

Using the picture of the various Kinds of cells found in people ask students to label the cells. Wide variety of free educational coloring pages available at: http://pinterest.com/genamayo/homeschooling-biology/

Also see supplemental page for various human cells.

Emphasize that God ordained that each plant, fish, animal and human cell would be distinct from the other. Muscle cells are muscle cells and nerve cells are only nerve cells. Liver cells never become skin cells. Clearly, the diagram shows they are distinctively separate from each other.

A human kidney can be transplanted into another human, but a horse kidney cannot be transplanted into a human, or a cow or a pig. A horse kidney can be only transplanted into a horse.

Activity: Gather a piece of fruit for each child. Have the student peel their piece of fruit, and place the piece on a paper towel to be examined under the microscope.

Craft Time:

As each student examines their piece of fruit under the microscope, engage the other children with the following animal craft.

1. Provide materials to make a pretend animal from. Each animal should be a unique material. For example, Pike Cleaners to make an elephant, pop sickle sticks to make a horse, cotton balls for making a sheep. The point is that each animal should be made from a different material. Glue eyes on the animal using a package of craft eyes.
2. Go to http://www.dltk-kids.com/animals/index.html for ideas of different "kinds" of animals and materials to make them from.

God, Our Creator
It's Show & Tell Time

Make a banner that says: "In the beginning God Created" and pin it to the bulletin board.

Beginning Activity: Have the kids cut out pictures from magazines to be used to illustrate the lesson.

As the story proceeds choose a child to come up to the table, pick an appropriate picture and tape it onto the board. (Comprehension test).

Have the kids hold their "creation" project they made last week for Show & Tell.

Now that we have made something,
Let's consider the work we put into it.

Did you slop through it, or did you carefully make your play like animal?

Show & tell the class what you made. Are you pleased with what you made? Did you do a good job? If a piece got broken or fell off could you fix it?

Did you toss it in the trash? Did you show it off?

Let's find out how much greater we are (God's Creation) than our little project?

Scripture Look Up:
Psalms 139:14 - 17

Mathew 10:29, 30, 31

Genesis 1:26, who made "man"? (Us – more than one; John 1:1-3);

What did man look like? (God)

How many think God looks like an ameba?

God's Word says HE made us to look like HIM, So, how could God have made us to look like an ameba? (He couldn't and He didn't)

God has a hand and an Ear (Isaiah 59:1) Show me your hand, show me your ear.

You DO NOT look like an ameba! So, God must not look like an ameba!

We know what we look like, so we have a basic idea of what God looks like.

We have 3 parts. We have a Body, Soul and a Spirit. (Genesis 2:7)

1:27 Did God make boys and girls at the same time? (Yes)

28, did God give His Creation a JOB? God wants us to take care of the world he gave us. How can we do that? (Even a child can pick up trash and be kind to animals.)

29 Did God give His Creations something to eat, or did He leave us to Starve? (See how God took care of us from the very beginning?)

30 How did God take care of His lower animal creation? (Appointed us to watch after them, gave them food to eat)

31 Was God, like you, really happy with His creation?

Magazine Pictures:
1. Men
2. Women (Babies too)
3. Trees
4. Animals (both baby and grown up)
5. Birds
6. Water
7. Sunshine
8. Moon
9. Stars
10. Clouds

11. Sky

12. Flowers

13. Grass

14. Bugs

15. Fish

Game Time: *DEFEND YOUR CHOICE*

TRUE or FALSE

Make a sign that reads True and one that reads False

Hand the signs on opposite sides of the room

Students run from one sign to the other according to the truthfulness of the following ideas:

1. God created the World TRUE
2. All birds can fly   FALSE – penguins cant fly
3. Even though the Bible says there are mountains in the bottom of the Ocean, science has proven that is not true. FALSE – there are mountains at the bottom of the ocean
4. Bear babies are called cubs   TRUE
5. H2o means oxygen   FALSE (water)
6. Links babies are called kits   TRUE
7. Hydrogen gas can be extracted/pulled out of water TRUE – through electrolysis
8. Lion babies are called cubs TRUE
9. Air has 4 different parts, but our body only uses 1 of them   FALSE (Air only has 3 parts: Nitrogen, Oxygen and Argon)
10.   Geese are called geesys FALSE (goslings)
11.   Wolves babies are called pups TRUE
12.   Beasts of the earth were made on the same day as people TRUE
13.   Oak tree seeds are called acorns TRUE
14.   Snow flakes are all the same FALSE

15. Baby horses are called pony's FALSE (colts) Ponies such as Shetland can be adults
16. Atmosphere means rounded TRUE
17. The Bible says there were Angels standing at the 4 corners of the earth, so that must mean the earth is square? (North/South & East/West)
18. Adam and Eve were told to name the animals FALSE (Only Adam)
19. God created land then filled up part of it with water FALSE – water came first
20. Scripture says the Sun, and Moon are the "greater lights" TRUE
21. The Ort Cloud is though to be the mother of all stars (It's *theorized* to be the mother of all comets) False

22. Plants give off oxygen to help people breathe TRUE
23. When we are "evolved" a little more we will be stronger than even God. FALSE (people are actually getting weaker and weaker.) In the beginning, people lived to be over 100 years old. Methuselah lived to be 969 years old. Noah lived to be 950 years old. Genesis 9:29. (Methuselah was the son of Enoch and the grandfather of Noah.)
24. People give off carbon dioxide to help plants breathe TRUE
25. God's Word, the Bible, has a few minor mistakes in it FALSE

26. God told Hercules to hold the earth steady in the universe. FALSE (the Bible says, "the earth is hung on nothing" Job 26:7)
27. Dinosaurs are spoke of in the Bible. TRUE (called Dragons)
28. According to the Bible the World is not Millions of years old, but about 6 or 7 thousand years old. TRUE
29. The name of our galaxy is Uranius FALSE (milky way)

Challenge the students to defend their answers. This will help them to actually think through their position on the matter in question.

MIRACLES – GOD'S SUPERNATURAL POWER

Beginning Activity: Pair the kids up in sets of 2. Provide material and patterns for the students to make a yellow sun, and a white moon.

They can draw a face on their sunshine, or whatever they like. They can make fringe out of crepe paper or streams to represent the suns movement.

NEXT:
Have each child blow up a balloon. Then see if they can hop on one foot and try to keep their balloon up in the air at the same time. The object is for them to try to do 2 things at once. (Later we'll talk about how the world God created has always – from the beginning of time - done 2 things at once 24/7).

Scripture Look Up:
Isaiah 40:22 Tells us that the world is round. People who didn't read their Bible thought the world was flat until Magellan's expedition proved the world was round.

What is an axel? Show the axel on the toy truck.

Using A Globe show how the earth turns on its axis every 24 hours.

That is so we can have the "Evening & the Morning".
Earth's axis runs North and South.

We have a North Pole and a _____ Pole. (Use
a globe to show how the earth turns on it's axis).

East & West do not connect like North & South.
What did God say in Psalms 103: 12 ?
God does not connect our sins back to us if we truly
ask for forgiveness.

Talk about SIN. Name some sins (write them on the
board)

Talk about forgiveness. When Jesus forgives us of our
sins they are as far from us as the East is from the
West.

Erase the sins to demonstrate how our sins are wiped
away.

"Romans 3:23 For all have sinned, and
come short of the glory of God;"

Let's pray and ask Jesus to forgive our sins.

THE STARS WERE BORN: Genesis 1: 14-16

THE PRESENT: Gift-wrap up a package of Glow in the Dark Stars and put a pretty bow on it.

Tell the children the person who can explain "Deep Time" will get the present. Deep Time is a "millions and billions of years" concept that questions how – if the world is really only 6 or 7 thousand years old - like the Bible says – then how did God make the light from the stars shine on earth in just 6 days since starlight is millions of light years away?

Correct Answer: It was a miracle using God's supernatural power. Just like God created Adam as a mature adult, he made the universe likewise.

When the first student who gives the right answer is given the gift and opens it, explain that the man made stars must absorb God made light to be able to shine in the darkness. (Designate that the winner must share the stars with their classmates so everyone can go home with a glow in the dark star).

Turn out the lights and see if they glow in the dark.

The World Does 2 Things at Once.

It spins to give us day and night, and **it also rotates** around the sun to give us summer, winter, spring and fall.

Have the students look up Genesis 1:14-19 and write it on their suns. (you may wish to make up a sample of what the sun might look like)

Ask, how long does it take for the world to rotate all the way around the sun.   Genesis 1:14. (1 year)

Joshua 10:11-14 The day the sun stood still.

The sun moves around our Milky Way Galaxy at about 483,000 miles per hour.

Speed of Light: 670 million miles/hour

It takes 8 minutes for sunrays to travel from the sun to the earth.

With their "sun" costumes on have the kids hold their world in their hand at arms length and slowly turn in a complete circle.

Scientists say it's impossible for the world to suddenly stop spinning (rotating around the sun) because the oceans would be sloshing everywhere and drown everyone on earth.

The Bible doesn't say the world stood still – it says the Sun Stood Still.

God brought time into existence when He said, 'and the evening and the morning were the first day". Since God started time He can also STOP time.

Isn't it possible God simply stopped time and the natural result of that would be that the "Sun stood still"?

No one knows exactly how God gave Joshua an extra day, but we know that God created the sun, moon and stars and He can make them do whatever He tells them to do.

Miracles

Put a small plate of **5 little fish crackers** on the table and a clear jar filled with fish crackers. Jesus fed 5,000 people with just 5 fishes and two little loaves of bread, and He walked on water, and He raised Lazarus from the dead, so giving Joshua an extra day didn't take months, weeks and years of planning for God. He may simply have raised his hand – much like a traffic cop – TIME STOPPED, and the sun stood still as a result.

Give a testimony of how God performed a miracle in your own life. If you can't think of anything ask a member of your church to give their testimony of something miraculous that God has done in their life.

Some well meaning Christians try to explain how God did this miracle. Some say, an unknown planet came between the earth and the sun interrupting the earth's gravitational pull and slowed the earth's rotation down to a crawl, others say it was a meteorite.

I wonder, just how would Joshua have known the perfect moment that such a monumental event was going to happen in outer space?

I believe that God miraculously created time, and God may have, simply and miraculously stopped time, with the earth continuing on its rotation as normal – totally uninterrupted.

Regardless of *HOW* God caused the sun to stand still, we know that God's word is **TRUE,** and someway somehow HE did it.

Game Time:

Creation Pictionary: All parts of creation are ok. Use the marker board.

1. Adam
2. Eve
3. Sun
4. Moon
5. Stars
6. Trees
7. Horses
8. Cows
9. Water
10.   Mountains
    Once someone guesses what the artist drew they hand the marker over and go get a treat.

    Class dismissed

"Life is in the Blood"

Beginning Activity: Teach the children the hymn, "Nothing But the Blood of Jesus". An easy way to do this is to use it somewhat like a singing cheer. The kids' part is to sing, "Nothing But the Blood of Jesus" and the leader sings the rest. The leader will point to the students when it's their part. (If you don't know the song ask a senior to come and teach it to the class)

Leader: What can wash away my sin?
Kids: Nothing but the blood of Jesus
Leader: What can make me whole again?
Kids: Nothing but the blood of Jesus
Leader: Oh, precious is the flow that washes white as Snow, no other fount I know
Kids: Nothing but the blood of Jesus

Open the Lesson with Prayer

DISCUSSION TIME: (allow the children to color the circulatory system sheet as you discuss the following)

Let's Talk About Blood

1. What is Blood? Ask the students for their ideas to engage them.

The Bible told us thousands of years ago that, the Life of the flesh is in the blood. Leviticus 17:11. What is flesh? Without our blood we die.

Who is George Washington?

His doctors thought if they took out his blood he would get well. What do you think happened to G.W. when the doctor put blood sucking leeches all over G.W.'s body and those leeches sucked out all his blood? He died. Wouldn't it have been great if his doctor had read the Bible?

Ask: Was the doctor back then smarter than the Bible? Are scientists of today smarter than the Bible?

2. Where does blood come from?
Blood is made in our bones.

Teacher information: For a great, 3 or 4-paragraph article on how blood is produced go to this article by Sue Wilson
http://www.pbs.org/wnet/redgold/basics/bloodproduction.html

3. Where is it stored? Blood veins and arteries (Circulatory System)
4. How does the blood get from one part of our body to the other?
5. Name some things blood does?

6. Name some ways we might loose blood?   Proverbs 6:16-20

7. How can we get more blood? Our bodies can make blood and now, doctors can do what is called Transfusions. Explain blood transfusions in simple terms. For example, before doctors can take blood from one person and give it to another they must make sure the blood types must match. ASK: Who likes to make A's and B's at school? The most common blood types are: A+ B+, A-, B-, AB+ AB- and O+ and O- or/ ABO

O for outstanding. Give each child a chart to take home.

Know Your Blood Type Before You Need Blood

		YOU CAN RECEIVE TYPE							
I F Y O U A R E T Y P E		O+	O-	A+	A-	B+	B-	AB+	AB-
	O+	*	*						
	O-		*						
	A+	*	*	*	*				
	A-		*		*				
	B+	*	*			*	*		
	B-		*				*		
	AB+	*	*	*	*	*	*	*	*
	AB-		*		*		*		*

Scripture Look Up: Leviticus 17:11, Proverbs 6:16-20

Ask: Do Apes have the same blood types to humans?

 Dr. Bruce Rideout is a highly respected veterinarian at the San Diego Zoo's Institute for Conservation Research. In response to a question posed by a reader as to whether or not primates have the same or similar blood types as human beings, Dr. Rideout replied that the blood types of only a half dozen or so primates has even been studied as of 2007. He emphatically stated that apes and old world monkeys do not have the same blood types as humans, although he believes they are similar.

The original article can be found at: *Ask an Expert, ABC Science in Sydney, Australia*

http://www.abc.net.au/science/articles/2010/04/07/2866275.htm

In conclusion, Dr. Rideout conceded that although there are similarities in the blood types between humans and apes, the two species are definitely not compatible when it comes to performing blood transfusions between them.

God made people, animals, bugs and sea creatures with some life systems alike, yet other life systems very different.

For Example,
While humans have a closed blood system (meaning that the blood never leaves the network of arteries, veins and capillaries),

Some of God's creatures, such as insects, worms, clams and crabs have an open circulatory system.

Additionally, sea creatures, such as corals and jellyfish have no circulatory systems at all.

God knew exactly what He was doing when He gave land creatures legs and sea creature's fins, and fowl of the air wings. He gave each species exactly what they needed to survive.

Why does a lady spider like a gentleman spider? They like each other because they are the same kind of creature. Spiders don't marry stinkbugs, and horses don't marry alligators. NEVER in the history of the earth has a dog married a pig. That's one of the many scientific proofs we have that God's word, Genesis 1:24 is true. Animals marry their "own kind".

Science Time:

Allow the children to observe a collection different species of bugs, plants, cells, or whatever you can gather for them to examine – hopefully under a microscope. You may be able to borrow slides of different species from the school or public library. Maybe even the hospital????

Discuss the many differences in the specimens.

Game Time:

Lets Make a Stink Bug

1. Cut the picture of the Stink Bug apart into as many pieces as possible. For example, cut the legs off, the tentacles, the head, and so on.
2. Now enlarge each piece on a copier
3. Lay all the pieces on a table to be assembled during the game
4. Gather a piece of cloth to work as a blind fold
5. Tape to tape the pieces back together

This game is played similar to Pin the Tail on the Donkey, except the object of the game is to show how God did such a better job of putting the parts of the Stink Bug where they belong. Notice where the stinky part is located. That's NOT by accident - that is by design.

Each child will have a chance to be blind folded and gather up the right piece to be placed in the correct location in order to create a paper stink bug.

Onlookers may wish to coach the person who is trying to blindly construct a stinkbug.

This game demonstrates how even the little stinkbug would not have fared well if it had been made merely by chance

Evolution & Creation are both Points of View
(Neither can be proven)

Beginning Activity:

Using a refrigerator box (from an appliance store near you) to represent our "universe" attach or draw various designs of stars, moon, constellations, etc. on all 4 sides. Additionally place objects inside the box that are not visible to the students. The objects can be both large and small.

Place the box across the room from the students. You may want to line students up against the wall.

Give each student a tablet/clip board to write what they can see without physically moving their body. They can stretch side to side, and some on one end will see more than others, but that's ok.

Now pass binoculars around (use a timer so everyone gets a chance because likely they will have to share the binoculars).

The point is that we on earth have only a very limited ability to see what our world and universe looks like – even when we use the best technology available.

We will never completely see all there is to see of God's handiwork, but we do have the Bible and by faith, additional to what little we can actually figure out of His creation, we can trust God that he has created a wonderful world for his creation to live in.

Now let the students move around to look inside, as well as on the backside of the box to see all that they missed when they were restricted from their stationary position.

We all saw the same box, but not everyone saw the same thing. We had many different points of view, not a single person saw everything there was to see.

Scripture Lookup:

We must come to God through faith:

Hebrews 11:6

But without faith it is **impossible to please** him: for he that cometh **to God** must believe that he is, and that he is a rewarder of them that diligently seek him.

God will NOT be put under a microscope:

Ezekiel 20:3 Son of man, speak unto the elders of Israel, and say unto them, Thus saith the Lord God; Are ye come to enquire of me? As I live, saith the Lord God, I will not be enquired of by you.

Some people prefer lies over truth preferring to worship God's creation instead of Him:

Romans 1:25 Who changed the truth of God into a lie, and worshipped and served the creature more than the Creator, who is blessed forever. Amen.

Mark 13:22

For false Christ's and false prophets will rise and show signs and wonders to deceive, if possible, even the **elect**.

Discussion:

Discuss how the latest "scientific" discoveries are being interpreted according to the evolutionistic point of view. Cite some of the spins and lies being told to further evolution.

Game Time: To Tell The Truth

Pick out an object that can be held/hidden in a student's hand behind their back.

Have one-student be the "Judge" whereby they pick 3 other students to be their Panel.

The judge leaves the room.
The chosen panel stands side by side
One student holds the object but all the students pretend to be holding the object.

The judge returns to the room to guess which panel member has the object.

The judge is allowed to ask the panel members questions to determine if they have the object.

Trying to be as convincing as possible the panel members may simply reply, "I am supposed to say that I have the object".

The judge has to decide from the available evidence

Right or wrong whoever the judge picks that person becomes the judge. (play until all the kids have had a chance to be in the game)

TODDLER CHALLENGE

On Sunday (prior to this class) ask the pastor to announce that the children's church would like to invite all the smartest babies in the land (2 years old and under) and their mother to join us Wednesday night for cookies and milk.

Emphasize that the babies do not have to be members of the church, but they must be very, very smart. Ideally, each student will be assigned their own baby, so if you know any parents with babies please invite them to join us for this delightful, scientific experiment.

Opening Prayer: Ask a student to open with prayer

Beginning Activity:
Have each student prepare and bake a batch of cookies. (Babies may stay in the nursery until cookies are ready). Left overs can go home.

Discussion: While the cookies bake demonstrate that our ability to comprehend God and His genius compares to a baby understanding the recipe for chocolate chip cookies. Naturally, this is beyond their comprehension.

Regardless of how smart we are, God's wisdom and understanding is so much greater. His wisdom is higher as the heavens are above the earth.

We are the created – He is the Creator! Therefore, like the baby trusts us to give them a chocolate chip cookie that has been prepared for them with the utmost of care, we have too – in the end – must trust God with the part of creation that we don't understand as well. What we *DO* have to know is that the God who loves us made creation for us.

There is absolutely no scientific PROOF, nor should intelligent people believe, that humans came from monkeys, just because we don't understand glutathione.

What we do know: God's word is truth and true science will always match God's word. If science tries to "exalt itself against the knowledge of God" it's faulty, bogus and simply junk science. Do not believe it.

Scripture Look Up:

Isaiah 55:9
For as **the** heavens are **higher than the** earth, so are my ways **higher than** your ways, and my thoughts **than** your thoughts.

2 Corinthians 10:5

Casting down imaginations, and every high thing that exalteth itself against the **knowledge** of God, and bringing into captivity every thought to the obedience of Christ;

Evolution tries to "exalt itself against the knowledge of God…."

Have students team up and list as many of the Ingredients for Baked Goods as they can think of: Identify all the similar ingredients for cookies, cakes, candy, bread, corn bread and brownies. All these products have many of the same basic ingredients, yet are nowhere near the same product. Doesn't it make sense that the creatures that were formed out of the same ground on the same day would have some common elements in their bodies? Does it make sense that someone who doesn't like God would try to discredit him and His creation?

The ingredients isn't what separates the baked goods, it's the way they are put together, and that's the same thing with human, animal and plant life. The cellular instructions for human life are totally different than instructions for plant life.

Write a list of other Favorite Foods on marker board:
Jell-O
Ice Cream
Mashed Potatoes
Hot Dogs

Ask the class how well they would like some flour in their mashed potatoes, or ice cream?

God told each new creature to go and reproduce after his or her own kind. Genesis 1:24 & 25 and then, "… God saw that it was good"

Ask the students if they agree with God that His creation is, GOOD! Wouldn't it be gross to have flour in your Jello?

Ask:
1. Has anyone ever had an injured animal?
2. How easy is it to communicate with an injured animal?
3. Isn't it a blessing that our animals have similar body parts like us?
4. We know what an injured leg feels like and that makes it a lot easier for us to care for (have dominion over) the animals.

People are created in God's image. We are highly intelligent, complex and ever growing and changing individuals. We are eternal beings.

God is even MORE intelligent and complex. He will NEVER run out of ideas. He will always be smarter, kinder and above his creation.

For anyone or anything to try and "exalt themselves above the knowledge of God" would be like the very, very smart babies we just made cookies for challenging their parents and saying, 'I can hold my own bottle now so I'm taking over the keys to car and the bank account.

In such an instance it is clear that the baby forgot they're not even potty trained yet.

Evolution scientists – who seem to think they're smarter than God, the father – in reality, they're not even educationally potty trained compared to God.

They may know a lot, but they don't know more than God.

So, lets talk about a few of the things that we know for sure about God's creation. Using our 5 senses lets each one name a part of God's creation and then explain how we can prove it really exists. Touch, Sight, Smell, Taste, Hear.

Can we "prove" *how* God made it? (Not really)
Can evolutionist "prove" we evolved from a glob of goo? (Not really)

Beginning Activity:

Dot-to-Dot Christmas Party Mural
(To be hung on the wall during the Christmas Party)

Comprehension Test

Instructions:
1) Draw 7 Dot-to-Dot Picture sets in a square for each child to complete and decorate. For example:
   Star, Angel, Crown, Manger, present, Sheep, Cross
   Write one of the verses for each child to look up.
   (May need to use verse more than once)
2) Each child will color/decorate all 7 of their pictures
3) Each child will look up their verse in a hard copy of the Bible, and circle the picture or pictures referred to in their assigned verse
4) Each child will sign their name and stamp their thumb print beside their picture – Ask them to do a good job.....

SCRIPTURE LOOK UP:
1) Matthew 2:2
2) Mathew 2:10
3) Mathew 2:11
4) Luke 1:30
5) Luke 2:7
6) Luke 2: 12
7) Luke 2:15 and 16
8) Luke 2:7
9) Luke 14:27

Game Time:
Tape the Candy on the Christmas Tree (Played like "Pin the Tail on the Donkey" child is blind folded) Once everyone has taped a piece of candy on the tree the kids get to go back and remove a piece after they have read out loud their assigned scriptures.

Note:
We were utterly amazed at how creative our kids were when it came to decorating their pictures in their assigned square. Some added a Jesus to their cross, some drew shepherds tending sheep and a Christmas tree for the present to sit under.

Suppemental Pages

Supplemental Activity Pages are here to assist you in your efforts to deliver these lessons. It is expected that you will have additional materials, ideas and resources that will add to what you find on these pages.

THE REAL CHRISTMAS STARS

Supplies: Turbans using cloth wrapped baseball hats.

Junior Magi (Discuss how they became Wise Men)
Turbans
Vocabulary Words:

- **Stars** – What is a Star? How Many Stars Do You Think There is? 200 billion stars in our Galaxy the biggest is the Sun." Sun is a star, but the real Star of Christmas is Jesus God's Son. Jesus is the "Bright and Morning Star"
- **Planets** 8 planets that rotate around the Sun in our Galaxy (Biggest – Jupiter & Saturn) Mercury Venus Earth and Mars are smallest,
- **Galaxy** – Milky Way If we stacked one penny up for every galaxy in our universe the stack would be 120,000 miles high
- **Universe** – where Galaxies live like a bowl that holds all the galaxies
- **Constellations** - Patterns made by Stars. locate Orion using 10o method.
- Scientist estimate there are Stars in the heavens = 200,000,000,000,000,000,000,000 Pslm. 147:4 and the Bible says that God knows each one of their names.
- Go outside and use the laser lights and telescope

4. Scriptures:
   - Genesis 1:1,
   - Job 38:
   - Orion fist is 10o count up 30degrees to find Orion Job 9:9
   - Job 26
   - Psalm 40, 19, 89 and 113

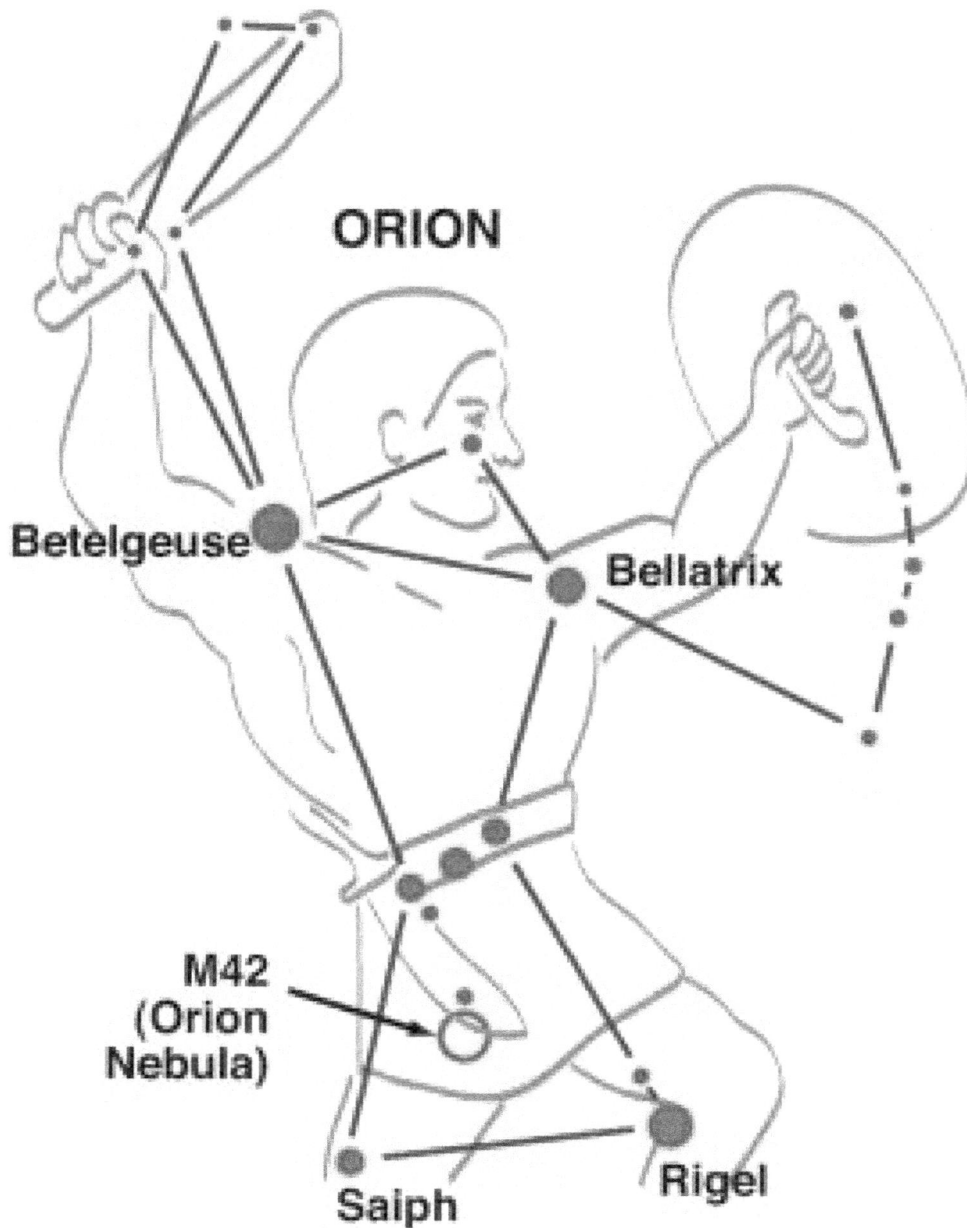

ORION

Betelgeuse

Bellatrix

M42
(Orion
Nebula)

Saiph

Rigel

Illustration From:
http://stardate.org/nightsky/constellations/orion

In the Bible: Amos 5:8

You and I are also a part of the Christmas Story. We take Jesus to the World – like Mary; we help tend God's little sheep – like the shepherds, we bring gifts to innocent children; and if we truly are Wise Men – we still seek, Jesus = the King of the Jews = savior!

Christmas Party 2013 Games

The Alphabet Game: The game starts off with one person saying, "A is for <u>angel</u> and B is for <u>baby Jesus</u>" and so on. Each letter in the alphabet should stand for something in the Christmas Story. If there are enough people there let the kids start the game and once they have gone through the alphabet, have the adults do the alphabet backward.

PICTURE GUESS: Divide the group up into teams of 4. Each team designates one person to be their artist. The artist comes up and draws a word out of the bowl and goes back to their group and starts to draw the word in picture form. The first group to get the word correct wins. The game can be extended by the team designating a new artist until everyone has had a turn at being the artist.

Gift Wrap Race
Each table is given wrapping paper, ribbon, tape and scissors

- First person goes to gift table choose a gift and a box it will fit in
- Pass the gift to someone on your right who will cut the wrapping paper
- Pass the gift to next person who will tape center together
- Pass to someone who will tape one end
- Pass to someone who will tape the other end

- Pass to someone who will put a ribbon on
- Pass to someone who will make and add the bow
- Pass to someone who will return the gift to the gift table
- The final person will unwrap the gift wearing mittens

Whichever table finishes first wins!
Prizes

Article from: Creation Magazine, September 2008.
Published by Creation Ministries International

http://creation.com/john-sanford

Plant geneticist: 'Darwinian evolution is impossible'

Don Batten chats with plant geneticist *John Sanford*

Plant geneticist Dr John Sanford began working as a research scientist at Cornell University in 1980. He co-invented the 'gene gun' approach to genetic engineering of plants. This technology has had a major impact on agriculture around the world.

Dr Sanford: 'As a new Assistant Professor, I was responsible for crop improvement. I worked on conventional breeding of fruit crops and became very familiar with the power of genetic selection and the limited range of changes that were possible through selective breeding. I soon became involved in plant genetic engineering research. At that time there were numerous genes which seemed potentially useful in crop plants, but there was no method for delivering these genes into the plant genome. There was no "transformation technology".

'I explored many gene delivery options before my colleague Ed Wolf (also of Cornell) and I came up with the idea of shooting DNA into cells, thereby penetrating cell walls and membranes. This initiated an exciting period of scientific exploration, involving many collaborating scientists from Cornell and other universities. In seven years the "gene gun" concept went from a laughable and crazy idea to an extremely effective gene delivery system. Almost all the early transgenic crops were transformed with the gene gun— especially corn and soybeans. A large fraction of today's transgenic crops were genetically engineered using our gene gun process.

'The gene gun has been only one of many areas of research for me. But it was this research that opened doors for me—providing recognition and financial resources.

'I look at the gene gun success as a special blessing that paved the way for my current work—which I consider much more significant.'

Dr Sanford was one of the scientists who developed the 'gene gun'. It fires genes into plant cells and revolutionized genetic engineering and plant breeding.
A change of mind

Dr Sanford was an evolutionist but changed his mind:

'I was totally sold on evolution. It was my religion; it defined how I saw everything, it was my value system and my reason for being. Later, I came to believe in "God", but this still did not significantly change my intellectual outlook regarding origins. However, still later, as I began to personally know and submit to Jesus, I started to be fundamentally changed—in every respect. This included my mind, and how I viewed science and history. I would not say that science led me to the Lord (which is the experience of some). Rather I would say Jesus opened my eyes to His creation—I was blind, and gradually I could see. It sounds simple, but it was a slow and painful process. I still only see "as through a glass, darkly" [1 Cor. 13:12]. But I see so much more than I could before!

'On a personal level this was a time of spiritual awakening, but professionally I remained "in the closet". I did not feel I could defend my faith in an academic setting. So I felt the need to take temporary leave from academia and institutional science because of the tension I felt in this regard, and the enormous potential hostility I sensed from my academic colleagues.

'I think the academic environment is very hostile to the very idea of a living and active God, making it almost impossible for a genuine Christian to feel open or welcome. I needed some distance from academia to get a hold of my own beliefs and why I hold them. I feel I have now grown to the point where I can re-enter institutional academia (to the extent that I am not expelled), without compromising my basic Christian beliefs.'

Is evolution important to science?

I asked John what he thought of the necessity of evolution for doing biological research.

Images from stockxpert/stock.xchng

Almost all the early transgenic crops were transformed with the gene gun—especially corn and soybeans.

'Institutional science has systematically "evolutionized" every aspect of human thought. Contrary to popular thinking, this is not because evolution is central to all human understanding, but rather has arisen due to a primarily political and ideological process. Consequently, in the present intellectual climate, to reject evolutionary theory has the appearance of rejecting science itself. This is totally upside down.

'An axiomatic statement often repeated by biologists is: "Nothing makes sense in biology, except in the light of evolution". However, nothing could be further from the truth! I believe that apart from ideology, the truth is exactly the opposite: "Nothing makes sense in biology except in the light of design".

'We cannot really explain how any biological system might have "evolved", but we can all see that virtually everything we look at has extraordinary underlying *design*.

'I am not aware of any type of operational science (computer science, transportation, medicine, agriculture, engineering, etc.), which has benefited from evolutionary theory. But after the fact, real advances in science are systematically given an evolutionary spin. This reflects the pervasive politicization of science.'

John explained how mutations, which supposedly provide the new genetic information to make evolution possible don't do the job:

'Mutations are word-processing errors in the cell's instruction manual. Mutations systematically destroy genetic information—even as word processing errors destroy written information. While there are some rare beneficial mutations (even as there are rare beneficial misspellings),[1] bad mutations outnumber them—perhaps by a million to one. So even allowing for beneficial mutations, the net effect of mutation is overwhelmingly deleterious. The more the mutations, the less the information. This is fundamental to the mutation process.'

Does natural selection help?

Dr Sanford: 'Selection does help. Selection gets rid of the worst mutations. This slows mutational degeneration.

'Additionally, very rarely a beneficial mutation arises that has enough effect to be selected for—resulting in some adaptive variation, or some degree of fine-tuning. This also helps slow degeneration. But selection only eliminates a very small fraction of the bad mutations. The overwhelming majority of bad mutations accumulate relentlessly, being much too subtle—of too small an effect—to significantly affect their persistence. On the flip side, almost all beneficials (to the extent they occur) are immune to the selective process—because they invariably cause only tiny increases in biological functionality.

'So most beneficials drift out of the population and are lost—even in the presence of intense selection. This raises the question—since most information-bearing nucleotides [DNA 'letters'] make an infinitesimally small contribution to the genome—how did they get there, and how do they stay there through "deep time"?

'Selection slows mutational degeneration, but does not even begin to actually stop it. So even with intense selection, evolution is going the wrong way—toward extinction!'

Dr Sanford has written a book: *Genetic Entropy and the Mystery of the Genome.*

Selection slows mutational degeneration, but does not even begin to actually stop it. So even with intense selection, evolution is going the wrong way—toward extinction!—Plant geneticist Dr John Sanford

'My recent book resulted from many years of intense study. This involved a complete re-evaluation of everything I thought I knew about evolutionary genetic theory. It systematically examines the problems underlying classic neo-Darwinian theory. The bottom line is that Darwinian theory fails on every level. It fails because: 1) mutations arise faster than selection can eliminate them; 2) mutations are overwhelmingly too subtle to be "selectable"; 3) "biological noise" and "survival of the luckiest" overwhelm selection; 4) bad mutations are physically linked to good mutations,[2] so that they cannot be separated in inheritance (to get rid of the bad and keep the good). The result is that all higher genomes must clearly degenerate. This is exactly what we would expect in light of Scripture—with the Fall—and is consistent with the declining life expectancies after the Flood that the Bible records.'

'The problem of genetic entropy (genomes are all degenerating), is powerful evidence that life and mankind must be young. Genetic entropy is probably also the fundamental underlying mechanism explaining the extinction process. Extinctions in the past and in the present can best be understood, not in terms of environmental change, but in terms of mutation accumulation. All this is consistent with a miraculous beginning, a young earth, and a perishing earth—which "will wear out like a garment" (Hebrews 1:11). Only the touch of the Creator can make all things new.

'All of the problems with evolutionary theory, as outlined in *Genetic Entropy and the Mystery of the Genome*, have now been rigorously proven using numerical simulation. We did this using "Mendel's Accountant", a state-of-the-art computer analytical tool for genetic systems. Five scientists—John Baumgardner, Wes Brewer, Paul Gibson, Walter ReMine, and I—developed this tool. We reported these new findings in two secular publications, and they will soon be discussed in a second book, *Genetic Entropy and Mendel's Accountant.'*

Dr Sanford also sees great potential for creation researchers:

'There is a desperate need for more creation researchers. The fields are white and ready for harvest, but the workers are very few [John 4]. Although there are thousands of creation-believing scientists and engineers, there is very little original research being done that significantly impacts the creation issue. Mainstream funding patterns, ideological presuppositions, and ideological filters ensure that almost all origins-related research will continue to beat the Darwinian drum. Bright, independently-minded scientists are desperately needed to swim against the current, critically examining all the Darwinian assumptions, and analyzing raw data for themselves. Even as I have found that evolution's "Primary Axiom" (i.e., mutation plus selection created all higher life functions) is demonstrably false, so there are many other "sacred cows" waiting to be de-throned.

'I believe the Lord is saying, "Whom shall I send?"'

CELLULAR LEVEL

Cell = Cell Phone (almost like the cellphone ☺, the basis of human life)

All cells (except red blood cells which lack a cell nucleus and most organelles to accommodate maximum space for hemoglobin) possess DNA, the hereditary material of genes, and RNA, containing the information necessary to build various proteins such as enzymes, the cell's primary machinery. There are also other kinds of biomolecules in cells.

Karyote = Karaoke   (Ask, who knows what Karaoke is)
   1. **Eukaryote** = You doing Karaoke (All multicellular organisms are eukaryotes, including animals, plants and fungi.)
   2. **Prokayote** = bad guys (bacteria) (a group of organisms – mostly unicellular- whose cells lack a membrane-bound nucleus). All their intracellular water-soluble components (proteins, DNA and metabolites) are located together in the same volume enclosed by the cell membrane, rather than in separate cellular compartments.

DNA = Do Not Argue (gives the orders that must be obeyed. It has our identification record. The color of our hair, skin, eyes and whether God wants us to be tall or short and whether we are a boy or a girl)

RNA = REALLY NICE ANGEL (has lots of important jobs like taking secret DNA messages all over the cell)

Tonight we're going to talk about how God created people as Eukaryote organisms.

Our Genetics (Genes) is what the DNA is talking about when it gives out the orders inside our cells.

We all start out as small as a dot like a period. Inside that tiny dot is over 6 feet of DNA with our complete identification. Dr. Gary Parker (ISBN: 978-0-89051-492-40) pp. 20

Eukaryote means the cells in our bodies, and the cells in the plants that God gave us to eat all have a wall/membrane around the nucleus that has our DNA to protect WHO WE ARE! We're individuals.

Prokaryote are bacteria's that have NO walls around any of the things inside their cells. They are ugly, and look like this:

God protects people and plants from prokaryotes (bacteria) using the wall/membrane he placed around the nucleus that holds our genetic identification, that's so that the prokaryote has a lot harder time making us sick.

Although they have absolutely NO proof, evolutionist believe that over billions and billions of years the bacterial organism, Prokaryote became a human, eukaryote, but that is impossible according to Dr. John Sanford who invented the Gene Gun.

Dr. Sanford figured out a way to shoot through the wall of plants and animals to add what he thinks is helpful to make plants and people safer from disease.

Dr. Sanford and a whole lot of other really smart scientist believe the world is not billions and billions of years old, but is less than 10,000 years old.

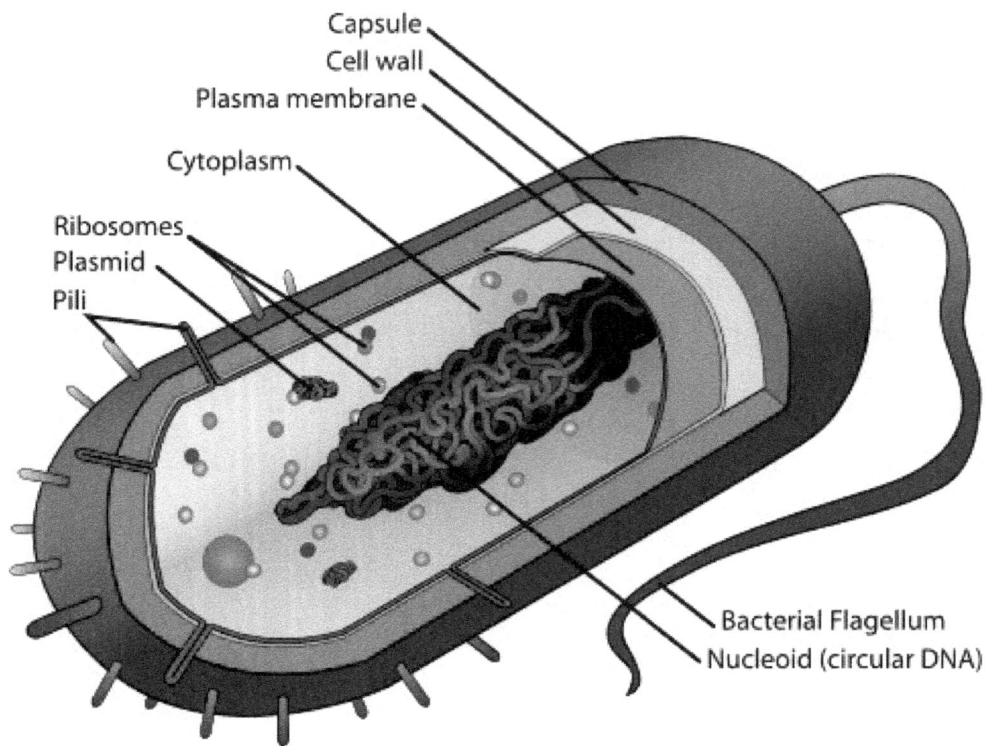

Capsule
Cell wall
Plasma membrane
Cytoplasm
Ribosomes
Plasmid
Pili
Bacterial Flagellum
Nucleoid (circular DNA)

Prokaryote illustration from:
http://en.wikipedia.org/wiki/Cell_nucleus

Article from: http://en.wikipedia.org/wiki/Eukaryote

A **eukaryote** (/juːˈkæri.oʊt/ or /juːˈkæriət/) is any organism whose cells contain a nucleus and other structures (organelles) enclosed within membranes. Eukaryotes are formally the taxon **Eukarya** or **Eukaryota**. The defining membrane-bound structure that sets eukaryotic cells apart from prokaryotic cells is the nucleus, or nuclear envelope, within which the genetic material is carried.[1][2][3] The presence of a nucleus gives eukaryotes their name, which comes from the Greek εu (*eu*, "well") and κάρυον (*karyon*, "nut" or "kernel").[4] Most eukaryotic cells also contain other membrane-bound organelles such as mitochondria or the Golgi apparatus. In addition, plants and algae contain chloroplasts. Many unicellular organisms are eukaryotes, such as protozoa. All multicellular organisms are eukaryotes, including animals, plants and fungi.

Cell division in eukaryotes is different from that in organisms without a nucleus (Prokaryote). There are two types of division processes. In mitosis, one cell divides to produce two genetically identical cells. In meiosis, which is required in sexual reproduction, one diploid cell (having two instances of each chromosome, one from each parent) undergoes recombination of each pair of parental chromosomes, and then two stages of cell division, resulting in four haploid cells (gametes). Each gamete has just one complement of chromosomes, each a unique mix of the corresponding pair of parental chromosomes.

Plant geneticist, and Cornell University scientist, Dr. John Sanford says, "Darwinian evolution is impossible". Dr. Sanford invented the Gene Gun, which helps (revolutionized) scientist make more food for the world.

Wikipedia: The gene gun was originally a Crosman air pistol modified to fire dense tungsten particles. It was invented by John C Sanford, Ed Wolf and Nelson Allen at Cornell University,[1][2][3] and Ted Klein of DuPont, between 1983 and 1986. The original target was onions (chosen for their large cell size) and it was used to deliver particles coated with a marker gene.[4] Genetic transformation was then proven when the onion tissue expressed the gene.

Dr. Sanford also states, "I am not aware of any type of operational science (computer science, transportation, medicine, agriculture, engineering etc.), which has benefited from evolutionary theory. But, after the fact, real advances in science ae systematically given an evolutionary spin. This reflects the pervasive politicization of science."

The **human genome** is the complete set of genetic information for humans (*Homo sapiens*). This information is encoded as DNA sequences within the 23 chromosome pairs in cell nuclei and in a small DNA molecule found within individual mitochondria. Human genomes include both protein-coding DNA genes and noncoding DNA.

Lesson 7
NATURAL SELECTION GAME

1. Make the longest word you can think of using the letters below
2. Make the second longest work you can
3. Continue to make new words discarding at least one letter with each new word until you can no longer discard a letter
4. The person who makes the most words wins a prize

The purpose of the game is to show that we can use all the letters to make new words, but eventually we will run out of letters and can make no more words, thus the game will be over. The same is true with natural selection. Natural selection is a matter of discarding bits and pieces of information to bring adaptation. Some scientist believes, natural selection could well explain how some animals become extinct.

Natural selection REMOVES information to help a species adapt to its new environment. Evolutionist claims that natural selection proves evolution. However, if you take their prokaryote (one cell bacteria) and start taking properties away the chances that it would have gone from a dead molecule to a highly organized and living person is mathematically impossible.

The Natural Selection Game
(You May Want to Enlarge Letters)

A b c d e f g H I j k l
m n o p q r s t u v w
x y z n l o p a I e o u
z r s t a m e n I w n b
o m c v u a q u s t

Did it take a lot of hard work for you to organize
these letters into a few words? Isn't it wonderful that
it only took God our creator, one day to organize the
many parts of our body into a live human being? We
are indeed, "fearfully and wonderfully made."

Science will NEVER prove that God did not make us.
1. He did make us 2. Somebody had to come up with
the idea and make up a plan to create our universe
and the people who live in it.

Article from:

"The Day The Sun Stood Still," by Eric Larabee was published in Harper's in January of 1950. It was reprinted in the Minneapolis Sunday Tribune on February 5 of that year, with the comment that "The article on this page--'The Day the Sun Stood Still'--will quite probably become the most discussed magazine piece of 1950. It was published in the current issue of Harper's Magazine, and the Tribune is the first newspaper to reprint it. The account is based on a book, Worlds in Collision, by Dr. Immanuel Velikovsky. The article has created such interest in publishing circles that, the Tribune has learned, the editors of Collier's and of The Reader's Digest have other presentations of the same idea in preparation. This Week magazine, which is a section of the Sunday Tribune and twenty- five other Sunday newspapers, is preparing a pictorial presentation of some of Velikovsky's unusual theories which lace together elements of religious beliefs and scientific events and try to explain that once--within the recorded history of man--the sun stood still." 5

Another indication of the trustworthiness of Joshua 10:13 can be found in astronomical data. It appears that one full day is missing in our astronomical calculations. On different occasions, Sir Edwin Ball, the great British astronomer, and Professors Pickering of the Harvard Observatory, Maunders of Greenwich, and Totten of Yale have traced this back to the time of Joshua. If we disregard calendar changes and deal only with a chronology based upon solar motion, and go back to the earliest available records, and trace the calendar through to the time of Joshua, the day of Joshua's battle was on a Tuesday, whereas if we compute backwards to the time of Joshua from the present day, the day of the battle would have been on a Wednesday. The day of the month is the same, but it is a different day of the week. In other words, if we reckon from the first recorded solstice in the ancient Egyptian records, the day is Tuesday, but if we reckon back from the most recent solstice, the day is Wednesday. These facts are extensively corroborated with astronomical data by Charles A. L. Totten in Joshua's Long Day, and the Dial of Ahaz (New Haven: Our Race Publishing Co., 1890). These facts came to widespread public attention in the late 1960's, after Mary Kathryn Bryan published an article in the Evening Star of Spencer, Indiana, about Harold Hill, President of the Curtis Engine Company in Baltimore, Maryland, a consultant to NASA at the Goddard Space Flight Center in Greenbelt, Maryland. According to the article, computer calculations bearing upon the positions of the sun, moon and planets were not coming out properly. These calculations were necessary, and had to be exact, in order to lay out the orbits of satellites and manned space flights. However, once the long day of Joshua and the retreat of the sun backward ten degrees in II Kings 20:9-11 were taken into account, all of the calculations worked out perfectly. This article was widely quoted, and copies of it appeared in many places for several years. Harold Hill later published his own account of these events in the thirteenth chapter of How To Live Like A King's Kid, which was substantially the same as that in Kathryn Bryan's article. In his account, he wrote: Later, someone sent me a clipping . . . saying I had admitted the whole thing was a hoax. Shortly thereafter, numerous religious magazines, some of them Christian, began repeating the false "retraction" and apologizing for their original participation in the rerun of the article. Not one of them ever checked with me as to the truth or error of the article as originally published. For the record--the report is true, the retraction false. . . . The whole sequence of events has demonstrated to me how prone even Christians are to believe a lie instead of the truth. 7

In an appendix to this chapter, Hill published a review of Totten's book written by V. L. Westberg, who stated: While Mr. Totten suggests an intervening comet perhaps caused the slow day by cutting off actinic rays, I feel a more realistic theory is to examine the possibility of a huge meteor or asteroid plunging into the earth's mantle slowing it down about one revolution while the inner molten core continued to rotate and eventually pull the mantle back in speed.

Mr. Totten recounted how Newton demonstrated how the earth could be suddenly slowed down without appreciable shock to people.

I have examined several maps of the Pacific Ocean which lend support to this theory.

The October 1969 map in National Geographic Magazine shows a large sink area between Hawaii and the Philippines with long fracture lines in the ocean bottom radiating outward to the continents.

The effect of such a crash would be maximum there at the equator on slowing the earth and would result in huge tidal waves which might help explain Dr. Northrup's studies on California's sand deposits. The size of the asteroid needed to slow down the earth one revolution could be calculated if mantle thickness were known and it could have been as large as Ceres--480 miles diameter.8

1 David Nelson, The Cause and Cure of Infidelity (New York: American Tract Society, 1841), pp. 26-27.

2 T. W. Doane, Bible Myths and their Parallels in Other Religions, fourth ed. (New York: Charles P. Somerby, 1882), p. 91.

3 Harry Rimmer, The Harmony of Science and Scripture (William B. Eerdmans Publishing Co., 1940), pp. 269-270.

4 Immanuel Velikovsky, Worlds in Collision (New York: The Macmillan Company, 1950), pp. 45, 46.

5 Quoted by O. E. Sanden, Does Science Support the Scriptures? (Grand Rapids, Mich.: Zondervan Publishing House, 1951), p. 9.

6 Ibid., p. 10.

7 Harold Hill, How To Live Like A King's Kid (Plainfield, NJ: Logos International), p. 71.

8 Ibid., p. 76.

Bottle Nosed Pig

Materials:
2 Liter Soda Bottle
4 egg carton cups for legs
Eyes
Paper Ears
Pipe Cleaner for the tail
Paint/Wrapping paper

1. Paint or wrap an empty soda bottle from one end to the other.
2. Glue the legs on.
3. Curl the pipe cleaner for the tail and attach to back of bottle
4. Glue the eyes on
5. Optional (put a few pieces of candy inside the "nose" of the bottle)
6. Paint the cap pink and screw on to bottle.

LESSON - 6

Hand Project – Use different colored construction paper to construct and demonstrate the tree of good and evil.

CREATION SCIENCE EXPERIENCES
By
_____

1. EXERIENCE A PITCH BLACK DARK ROOM: "And the earth was without form and void; and _____ was upon the face of the deep. And the spirit of God moved upon the face of the _____. Genesis 1:_____
What would you observe?_____

   What would you expect to touch?_____

   What might you hear?_____

2. Looking through a PRISM: God said, "Let there be_____ and there was _____. Genesis 1:_____
What would you observe?_____
_____

3. Do children have the same fingerprints as their parents? Yes No

4. "I am _____And _____made". Psalm 139:14

5. OXYDATION: To explain what happens to a peeled fruit or potato go to Mathew 6:19. Write your observations below:
_____

6. Can Creation Scientist see God?   Yes   No
John 1:18
Jesus said, "have _____ in God".   Mark 11:22

Can Evolution Scientist see the Oort Cloud?
Yes   No
Do Evolution Scientist believe there is an Oort
Cloud? Yes   No

Should Creation Scientist tell Evolution Scientist
they are *stupid* for believing in the Oort Cloud?
Yes No Why? Ephesians 4:32

Should Creation Scientist tell Evolution
Scientists that God is real?
        Yes   No   Mark 16:15

Are cupcakes good for children? Yes   No

HORSE CIRCULATORY SYSTEM

Veins and arteries

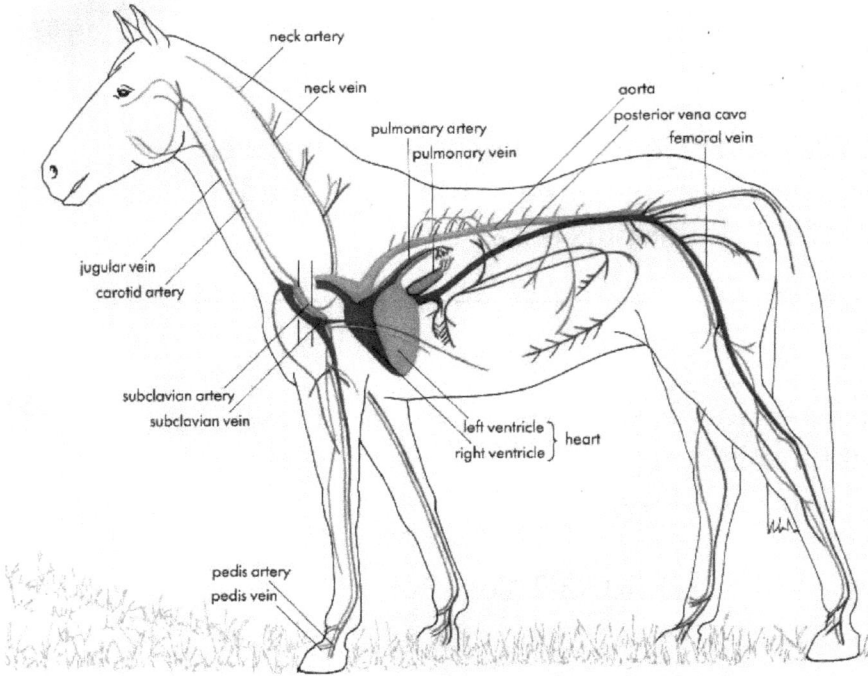

Illustration from:

Garden of Eden

One Word Riddle

What is more powerful than God? What is more evil than the Devil? Rich people have none. Poor people have too much, and God hung the earth on it. Job 26:7
(The answer has seven letters)

Answers for Bell Game is in Genesis 1:26-31, 2:8-17

Questions: 1. God told man to rule over certain parts of creation. Can you name the things God allowed men to rule over?

2. What did God give to man for food?

3. God saw all that He had made and it was very _____ ?

4. The trees in the garden were _____ to the eye and good for _____.

5. Where did God put the man He had created?

6. Name one of the four rivers that flowed from the Garden of Eden.

7. What job did God give man?

8. God told Adam and Eve that they could eat from all trees but one, which tree did God tell Adam and Eve that they could not eat from?

9. How can we know good from evil?

_____

"One Day is as a Thousand Years"
2 Peter 3:8

"…and the evening and the morning were the first day". Genesis 1:5 There is your timetable for the earth. Because where God lives is eternal, …to **_God,_** one day *IS* as a thousand years…. But for people on earth, one day is 24 hours.

God created the earth for **_people,_** and gave us plants to eat and animals to take care of. He knew we would get bored just sitting around, as well as the fact that animals were not created to be as intelligent as people, and therefore would need a zookeeper.

God knew we could not stay awake 500 years/day, and sleep 500 years, so He created the earth to have a arcadia cycle that would support plant, animal and human life. Otherwise, going 500 years/night without light the trees, people, and animals would all die off "overnight".

Evolutionist trying to reason/twist scripture to mean that one day to God could have been millions or billions of years is illogical. God knew who He was talking to when he said, "and the evening, and the morning were the first day".

DID YOU KNOW?

1. Scientists on both sides agree that there was a beginning. "In the beginning, God created the heavens and the earth" Genesis 1:1
2. The Bible says the World is a circle. Isaiah 40:22
3. The "Nebraska Man" evolutionist claimed to have found **Nebraska Man** which was a name applied to a putative species of ape. *Hesperopithecus* meant "ape of the western world," and it was heralded as the first higher primate of North America. *Haroldcookii* was given as the species name in reference to the original discoverer of the tooth, Harold Cook. It was originally described by Henry Fairfield Osborn in 1922, on the basis of a tooth that rancher and geologist Harold Cook found in Nebraska in 1917. The discovery was made around ten years after the finding of Piltdown Man, another possible human ancestor that turned out to be a hoax. Although Nebraska man was not a deliberate hoax, the original classification proved to be a mistake. Nebraska Man turned out to be neither man nor ape, but the tooth of a pig! (http://en.wikipedia.org/wiki/Nebraska_Man)
4. There has NEVER been a missing link that would prove evolution. There are no missing links between man and apes. Evolution is about funding for it's researchers, and can never be proven because it is a lie! DNA (Do Not Argue)

Illustration from:
http://foodfashionscience.blogspot.com

For edible DNA and cell ideas go here:
http://iijuan12.squidoo.com/cells-and-dna

Stink Bug

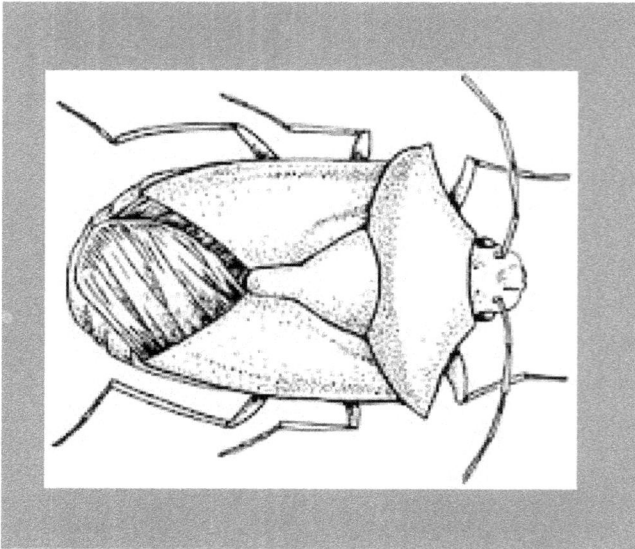

Illustration from:

World Oceans – Lesson 4

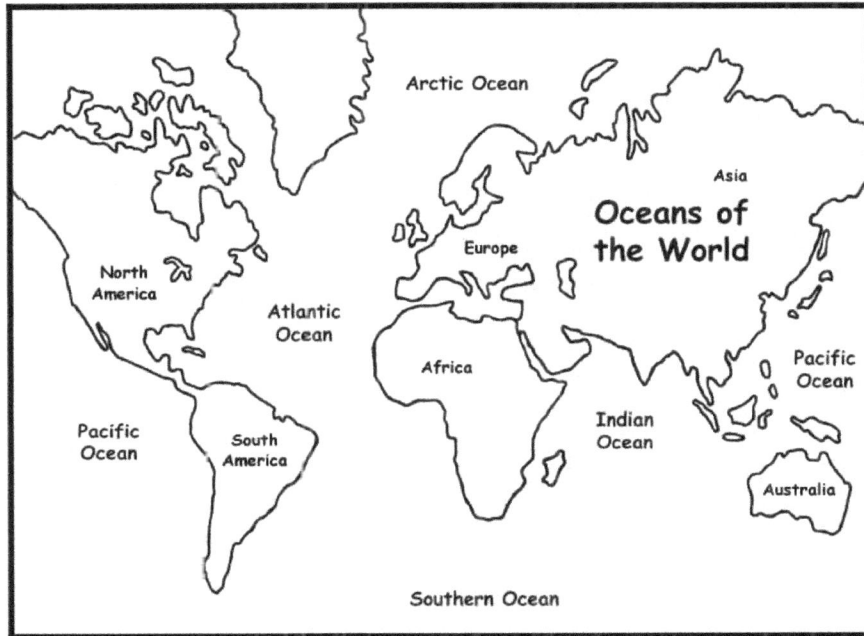

Oceans of the World

Arctic Ocean

Asia

Europe

North America

Atlantic Ocean

Africa

Pacific Ocean

South America

Indian Ocean

Pacific Ocean

Australia

Southern Ocean

Copy and enlarge as necessary

The Equator – Lesson 4

The *earth's equator* is an imaginary line that separates the Northern Hemisphere from the Southern Hemisphere. It's located halfway between the North Pole and the South Pole, is almost 25,000 miles long, and three quarters of it is over water.

Our summers and winters are due to the earth rotating around the sun, and the tilt of the earth's axis. The Northern and Southern Hemispheres take turns leaning to and away from the sun during this highly complex and magnificent process.

When the equator is discussed in general, people are referring to the *earth's equator*. However, few realize the "astronomical" impact that the equator has on creation vs. evolution. The truth be known, and it is not hidden, not only does the earth have an equator, but other planets and astronomical bodies do as well.

This one amazing fact screams intelligent design to most reasonable people. Psalms 19:1,2

> The heavens declare the
> Glory of God;
> And the firmament shows
> His handiwork.
>
> Day unto day utters speech,
> And night unto night
> Reveals knowledge

The equator
God's a-MAZE-ing Creation
Lesson - 4

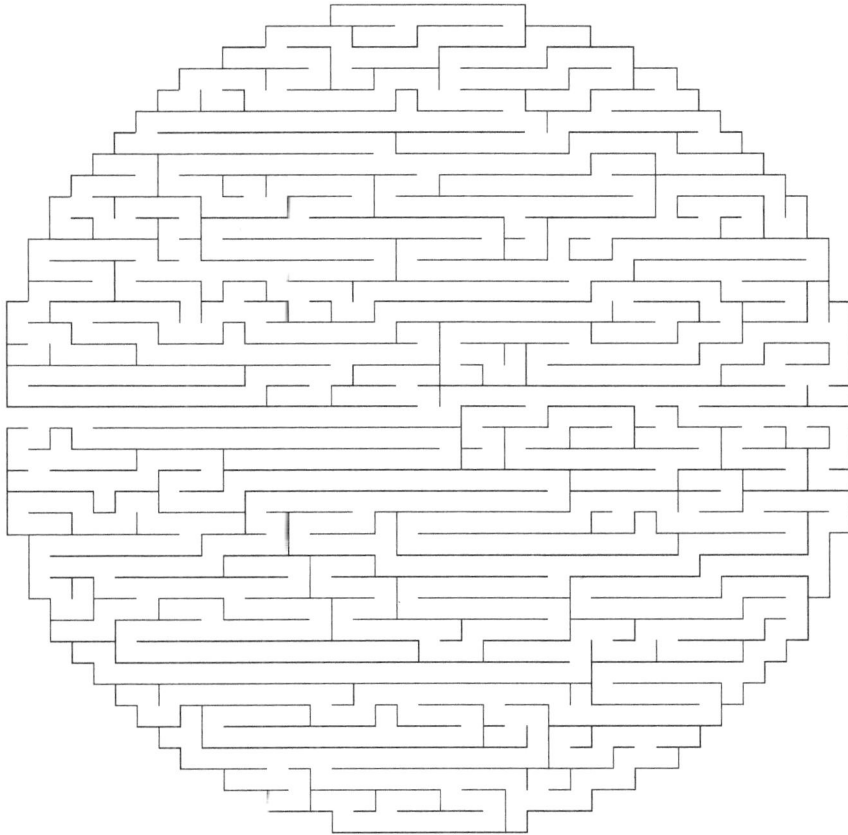

Created by Puzzlemaker at DiscoveryEducation.com

Copy and enlarge as necessary.

Creation Animals Coloring Page - Lesson 4

Copy and enlarge as necessary

Human body cells – Lesson 11

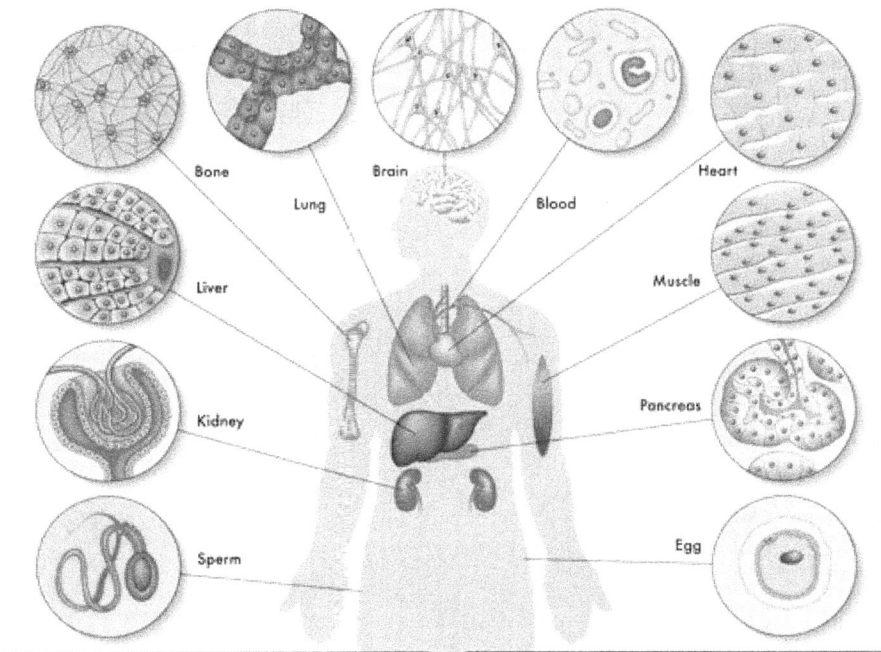

Copy and enlarge as necessary.

Name human cells – Lesson 11

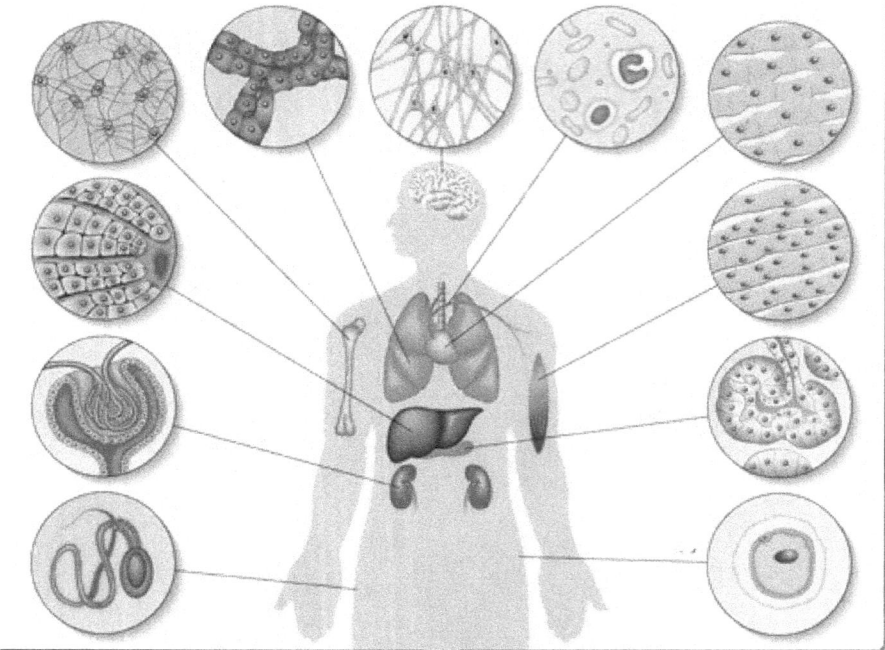

Copy and enlarge as necessary.

More Learning & Motivations Ideas
http://crosswisepublishing.com

Notes